What people are saying about …

I Am N

"There is no doubt that radical Islam is one of the greatest challenges facing the church today. These inspiring accounts of the persecuted church will move you to tears and then drive you to your knees. We all have a scriptural responsibility to stand up for and stand with our brothers and sisters who are going through the fire. Don't let the horrors described here intimidate you, because fear is a terrorist's greatest weapon. Instead, be stirred up to pray that the Holy Spirit may give you boldness to speak out, to take action, to get involved. Similarly, don't let these indescribable crimes fill you with hate for Muslims. Many Muslims would join us in condemning these atrocities. We are called to follow our Savior in loving our enemies, serving their needs, and having compassion on their blindness. The sacrificial faith of the suffering saints described in this book show us all how we are to respond at this time of crisis, courageously daring to love Muslims with the love of Christ."

Julyan Lidstone
Operation Mobilization (OM)

"VOM's *I Am N* is a challenging mosaic of stories that remind us of normal Christianity, faith that is lived out in persecution. There are a lot of reminders within the pages of this book. We are reminded that there are no such entities as a 'free church' or a 'persecuted church'; there is simply *one church*, always persecuted and free. The church in persecution teaches us how to pray, not that their persecution might end but that they might be obedient through their sufferings. This is a prayer that prays both halves of the prayer of Jesus. It is always appropriate to pray for 'let this cup pass' while never forgetting to pray to the Father that 'thy will be done.'"

Nik Ripken
International Mission Board (IMB) of the
Southern Baptist Convention
Author of *The Insanity of God* and *The Insanity of Obedience*

"Islamic terrorism is often the lead news story of the day, but Jesus promised to build his church and that the gates of hell would not prevail against it. So although terrorism grabs the headlines, Jesus's followers are flourishing right in the heart of the danger. *I Am N* was written to tell the stories of brave believers on the front lines of today's raging spiritual battle. Their courage will inspire you to think differently, live differently, and your heart will be refreshed as you get to know them. I believe they have become the new face of Christianity and we can learn much from them. The word *retreat* is foreign to the gospel. Brothers and sisters who live in harm's way today are in no way waving white flags. Instead, they're yelling 'Charge' and taking the gospel to the ends of the earth even if it costs them their lives."

Tom Doyle
e3 Partners
Author of *Killing Christians: Living the
Faith Where It's Not Safe to Believe*

"Instability is our new normal. The gospel must ever be preached under pressure, and we must give up the idea that we can truly stand up for Jesus anywhere in the world without suffering for him. The only people in the world who can avoid the equal and opposite errors of Islamophobia and naive accommodation are the followers of Jesus who love Jesus enough to share in his sufferings and who love Muslims enough to suffer and die for them."

Dick Brogden
Assemblies of God World Missions
Author of *Live Dead Joy: 365 Days of Living and Dying with Jesus*

"The further we are removed from the suffering of others, the easier it is to do nothing. We must not allow ourselves that option. Through these stories, please allow yourself to draw near to our persecuted brothers and sisters. In my role as a leader of a missions agency reaching out to Muslim people, I've been pulled into the suffering. Personal friends have been beaten, imprisoned, tortured, or killed. My tears, sleepless nights, and prayers didn't seem enough. I am extremely grateful for a partnership we now have with The Voice of the Martyrs. In practical ways they are helping us deal with the persecution and showing us how to get back up and press on with the good news of God's love through Jesus. This book will help us all respond in compassion."

Kevin
Missions executive with more than thirty years of
service in restricted and least-reached nations

"It has been our honor and privilege to pray, weep, and serve alongside brothers and sisters who have suffered for Christ at the hands of their families, neighbors, and governments. As we recall their faces and tell their stories, we join the apostle Paul in saying, 'I thank my God every time I remember you … I always pray with joy because of your partnership in the gospel from the first day until now' (Philippians 1:3–5). God is at work in extraordinary ways in the midst of the worst possible terror, oppression, and violence. The Christians you will meet in this book reveal a hope and strength that is both supernatural and eternal. These family members have completely abandoned their personal agendas and are learning to trust God absolutely. We have much to learn from their example."

Cole, Cheryl, and Jason
The Voice of the Martyrs
Executive editors, *I Am N*

i am n

the voice of the martyrs

i am n

*Inspiring Stories of Christians
Facing Islamic Extremists*

David C Cook

transforming lives together

I AM N
Published by David C Cook
4050 Lee Vance View
Colorado Springs, CO 80918 U.S.A.

David C Cook Distribution Canada
55 Woodslee Avenue, Paris, Ontario, Canada N3L 3E5

David C Cook U.K., Kingsway Communications
Eastbourne, East Sussex BN23 6NT, England

The graphic circle C logo is a registered trademark of David C Cook.

The website addresses recommended throughout this book are offered as a
resource to you. These websites are not intended in any way to be or imply an
endorsement on the part of David C Cook, nor do we vouch for their content.

Unless otherwise noted, all Scripture quotations are taken from the ESV® Bible
(The Holy Bible, English Standard Version®), copyright © 2001 by Crossway, a
publishing ministry of Good News Publishers. Used by permission. All rights
reserved. Scripture quotations marked KJV are taken from the King James Version of
the Bible. (Public Domain); and NKJV are taken from the New King James Version®.
Copyright © 1982 by Thomas Nelson. Used by permission. All rights reserved.

Details in some stories have been changed to protect
the identities of the persons involved.

LCCN 2015956834
ISBN 978-1-4347-0987-5
eISBN 978-1-4347-0997-4

© 2016 The Voice of the Martyrs, Inc.

Printed in the United States of America
First Edition 2016

1 2 3 4 5 6 7 8 9 10

121715

Remember them that are in bonds, as bound with them; and them which suffer adversity, as being yourselves also in the body.

Hebrews 13:3 KJV

Contents

The Story behind the Stories

"I am n?" What does that mean?

When militants from the self-proclaimed Islamic State of Iraq and Syria (ISIS) moved into northern Iraq, they began identifying Christian-owned property. Families would find the Arabic letter ن (*nun, noon*), or *n*, painted on their homes and churches. This single letter conveyed the powerful accusation that the occupants were "Nazarenes," people who followed Jesus of Nazareth rather than Islam.

To be labeled "n" in a community dominated by Muslim extremists is to undergo an immediate identity and life change. With this mark comes the ultimatum: If you convert to Islam or pay the tax, you can keep your material possessions and remain in this community. If not, leave or you will die.

Any person who takes a stand for Jesus in occupied Iraq, any person who chooses to be "n," pays a high cost. Without warning, some Christians are dragged from their homes and businesses by armed militants—and they are never seen again. Pastors who share the message of Jesus in their communities are beheaded in front of their families. Children who will not renounce Jesus are shot. Teenagers may be taken from their homes and families and forced into service to ISIS or beaten, mutilated, and left for dead. Other atrocities are so horrific we will not describe them here.

Since 2003, such persecution has forced more than a million Iraqi Christians, who refuse to renounce Jesus and the Bible, to flee. Many survivors live in refugee camps, trusting God daily for their food, shelter, and safety because they have no money, no work options, and no other place to go. Even more challenging is the reality that their situation is not temporary; their life circumstances on this earth are unlikely to improve—ever.

Yet their courageous, steadfast commitment to God in the face of persecution provides Jesus followers all over the world with a powerful picture of what being "n" is all about. They willingly sacrifice everything they have in this world in order to fulfill God's calling to obey and serve him. Like the heroes of the faith whose stories we read in the Bible and in the record of church history, they are living out Paul's words in Philippians 1:21: "For to me to live is Christ, and to die is gain."

Stories That Must Be Shared

This book was written in order to share the stories of Christians—from Nigeria to Malaysia to Pakistan—who have suffered persecution from Muslim extremists. As you read these stories, please understand that this book is not intended to encourage any hatred toward Muslims. Rather, we join our persecuted family in loving Muslims and working to see them come to Christ.

We want you to have the opportunity to get to know some of the persecuted Jesus followers who live in hostile communities and nations. Their stories matter because they are our brothers and sisters in the global family of Jesus Christ and they need us to stand with them. We, in turn, need their example of faithfulness in the face of persecution to encourage us in our walk with the Lord (Hebrews 12:1–2). Their sacrifices are a powerful testimony to our loving God, whose grace reaches out to save every sinner and empowers those who receive Jesus as Savior and Lord to live in faithful service to him.

It won't be easy to read these stories. Knowing that these true accounts of actual incidents happened to real people is unsettling. Some incidents are troubling at the least; others are truly horrifying. For every one of these stories, there are hundreds more that will never make the evening news or a Twitter feed.

We are sharing these stories through eyewitness accounts and interviews. They are not historical composites based on hearsay; they are current and real, having taken place between 2001 and 2015. We have eaten meals with these brothers and sisters in Christ, prayed with them, and helped to meet some of their needs. Although these narratives are true to actual events, some dialogue and descriptions are based on reasonable consideration of time, place, and circumstance. For obvious reasons, we use pseudonyms and may not mention specific locations or other particulars. Given the constraints of sharing stories such as these, this is the most accurate, complete, and realistic book we can offer about these modern-day witnesses for Christ.

Stories That Provoke Response

We share these firsthand stories so you will come to know your brothers and sisters who are being persecuted for their Christian faith. We invite you to look deeply into their eyes and allow yourself to share in their experience of faith as they live it out in their world. It may feel uncomfortable to do so. It may be tempting to look away, as we tend to do when we encounter the panhandler at the bus station or the homeless person holding up a cardboard sign at the traffic light. But if that person were a family member, a brother or sister, would we still look away? Or would we be drawn to embrace and help that person who faces great difficulties?

Our goal is not to elicit pity for persecuted Jesus followers in hostile Muslim countries. That is not why we share their stories. Our motive is simply to describe their experiences so you will stand with them. So you will pray for them. So they will know that they are not alone in their efforts to share the love of Jesus when doing so gets them—or their loved ones—beaten, tortured, or killed.

Our desire is for Christians around the world to recognize these persecuted followers of Jesus as their brothers and sisters in the family of God and to embrace them in that intimate unity: "Remember those who are in prison, as though in prison with them, and those who are mistreated, since you also are in the body" (Hebrews 13:3).

As we get to know these persecuted followers of Jesus, we discover that they are not "super Christians" who have somehow attained a higher level of godliness. They are people just like us. They feel deep anguish when their children are taken away, their husbands are killed, their sons are attacked, their wives are raped, and their daughters are forced into sexual slavery. They face uncertainty and fear when they are kicked out of their families, lose their jobs, and are cast out of their communities because they follow Jesus.

To thrive while enduring such suffering, they pray for courage, faith, and endurance. They tenaciously cling to the Word of God, trusting in the loving, faithful character of God and the certainty of heaven. Having lost everything of value in this world, they learn to trust that God is in control no matter what.

As our persecuted brothers and sisters in Christ walk this path, they begin to see their circumstances through God's eternal perspective. That perspective changes everything. It leads them to view themselves not primarily as the persecuted but as those who serve on the front lines as God accomplishes his purposes in the midst of evil and chaos. They don't focus their attention on their small minority; they focus on the majority of people who are reachable for Christ. Their eyes are open to see that ISIS or other Muslim extremists are not thwarting God's eternal plan.

The world is not just one big chaotic mess. God is at work powerfully and strategically. The very suffering of our persecuted brothers and sisters is creating a deep hunger for the truth of Jesus among many moderate Muslims who express deep hurt, regret, and even anger concerning the atrocities in Iraq. Some even say, "We've read the Quran and know that Muhammad himself committed such atrocities. Now we want to learn about Christianity—about Jesus, about the Bible. Please tell us more."

Seizing the opportunity, these precious followers of Jesus boldly proclaim, "I am n." Counting the cost, they stand firm, faithfully sharing the message of God's grace to a world that desperately needs him. How can we let them stand alone or suffer in silence? Will we let their stories deepen our commitment to Christ and his Great Commission? Will we say, "Count on me. I am n too"?

The Voice of the Martyrs

Part I

SACRIFICE

*And he said to all, "If anyone would come after me, let him
deny himself and take up his cross daily and follow me."*
Luke 9:23

The reality of making a personal sacrifice for one's faith isn't something most Christians in the West are forced to think about very often. For the most part, we can live comfortable lives, making plans for the future and pursuing our hopes and dreams. Yes, we make sacrifices along the way, but they often focus on sacrificing one thing we want for something we want even more—working extra hours so we can buy that new mountain bike, postponing buying a new car so we can take that trip we've always wanted to take, or giving up a tee time to go to the kids' soccer game. Of course, we sacrifice some of our time to volunteer and we financially support our favorite causes too.

Sacrifice is never far from the hearts and minds of Jesus followers who are persecuted by Islamic extremists. For them, the consequences of obedience to Christ are clear. The sacrifices they make are certain and well defined. Before they choose Jesus as Lord and Savior, they count the cost of being his disciple. They know that once their faith becomes visible to others, persecution will come. They expect it, and they accept it. They understand Paul's words in Romans 12:1 in a way few of us can: "I appeal to you therefore, brothers, by the mercies of God, to present your bodies as a living sacrifice." And they make that personal sacrifice every day.

They witness for Jesus in hostile communities rather than fleeing to safer countries—and are often arrested, jailed, beaten, tortured, or killed.

They prepare their children for persecution, and even martyrdom, as the consequence of living out their faith in Jesus.

They face daily beatings or even expulsion from their once-protective Muslim families through which all of life's opportunities flow: food, shelter, education, marriage, and work.

Their homes and possessions are confiscated or destroyed, driving them to live in refugee camps where they have nothing to call their own and no promise of food, shelter, or safety for tomorrow.

The depth of their sacrifices in order to serve Jesus faithfully is hard for us to comprehend if we haven't experienced such persecution. Yet our brothers and sisters who follow Jesus in Muslim countries proclaim, through word and action, "It's worth it. We are disciples of Jesus. We will remain committed to God and his kingdom no matter what sacrifices are required. We are called to make disciples. Regardless of what happens, we have hope because Jesus promised to prepare a place for us where we will be with him forever."

As you read the firsthand stories that follow, may God open your eyes to see the world in which your brothers and sisters choose to be "living sacrifices" for Christ. May he open your heart to love and stand with them.

1

The Day ISIS Arrived in Mosul

Abu Fadi
Iraq

The June 2014 day broke like almost any other day in Mosul, Iraq: hot and dusty and teeming with people, traffic, and trade. People flocked to marketplaces in Iraq's second-largest city (population 660,000). Horns honked amid the pent-up traffic. As the day progressed, the din of street-side chatter rose appreciably. By noon, it sounded like a cacophony of blackbirds chattering among themselves.

That's when Abu Fadi, a sixty-five-year-old Mosul native living just miles from the city, received the phone call that changed everything. For some, the phone call marked the beginning of the end of life as they knew it—and in some cases their very lives.

"Abu," said a friend in Arabic, "ISIS is coming. We have heard from someone we trust. Today is the day."

For weeks the rumor mill had been churning that self-proclaimed ISIS terrorists who had been ravaging cities elsewhere in Iraq would take Mosul next. That's where Abu's mother, Sara, and sister, Dleen, still lived. As Christians, they would be in grave danger. ISIS hated many people in the world, but especially Christians. The ultimatum to followers of Jesus? Convert to Islam, pay an outlandishly high tax, leave, or be killed.

"How can we hope to get my mother and sister out?" asked Abu. Both women were disabled and in wheelchairs.

"It will not be easy," his friend stated. "And if Mosul falls, can your city be far behind? We must pray very hard, Abu. We must—"

Baroom.

An ISIS military water tanker, rigged with explosives, blew up near the Mosul Hotel, where government security officers were stationed. Abu's friend hung up the phone. Chaos descended on Mosul.

Armored vehicles rumbled down streets. ISIS troops began freeing the first of what would be about one thousand prisoners. Gunfire broke out. A woman who had planned to celebrate this day as her wedding day died in a blast.

ISIS fighters ripped down the cross on the Syriac Orthodox cathedral of Mar (meaning "saint" or "martyr") Afram. They replaced the cross with loudspeakers proclaiming that Islam, not Jesus, was the way.

Everywhere chaos reigned. People dragged possessions to cars. Traffic jams closed roads. Screams of panic echoed. Amid it all, Abu received sporadic phone reports from his friend in Mosul, who at one point said, "The Iraqi army is now fleeing the city."

During the following weeks, Abu secured permission from an ISIS judge to permit his mother and sister to stay in Mosul. A few weeks after taking Mosul, ISIS swept into Abu's city, just as he had feared. More Christians hastily packed and fled, but Abu and his wife, Rukia, could not leave Sara and Dleen in Mosul.

For sixteen days, ISIS occupied the area where Abu lived—sixteen days that to Abu seemed like sixteen years.

"Please come get me, Abu," pleaded his mother during yet another phone call from Mosul. "It is not safe here. You must—"

A man's hardened voice cut in on the line. "Let me state it more clearly," the ISIS soldier declared. "If you do not come get these two infidel dogs, they will either be converted to Islam with guns at their heads or thrown onto the street."

Abu had no chance to get his mother that day because he'd be going against the surge of frantic people escaping the city. Both women were allowed to stay with a Muslim neighbor for the night, but the ISIS soldier confiscated their house, pulled a can of spray paint from a bag, and tagged the front of the house with ن—an Arabic *n* for "Nazarene"—*Christians live here. Property of the Islamic State.*

Unable to go to his mother and sister, Abu arranged for a Muslim friend to drive the women to him. Once they arrived, Abu and the women could flee from there. Like almost forty thousand others who fled the purge in Mosul and the surrounding area, they crammed the few possessions they could fit into the car and headed east for relative safety in the city of Erbil, sixty miles away.

Soon Abu and his family arrived at the first checkpoint. Cars weighed down to their struts with people and their possessions inched forward in dozens of lines. Exhaust stained the air. ISIS guards stood with firearms and swords. Abu had prayed about this moment—for courage to stand for his beliefs.

"Who are you?" a guard asked.

"We are Christians leaving Mosul, because we are not permitted to stay in this Muslim land," Abu replied.

The guard, now joined by others, refused to let the family pass. Instead, they placed a call to superiors. Thirty minutes later, two shiny SUVs arrived. Young men brandishing new, expensive firearms stepped out and began peppering the family with questions.

Abu answered honestly: "Yes, we are Christians."

"Leaving is no longer an option for you and the rest of your infidel family," said the leader. "Convert to Islam or be killed. It is that simple. It is an easy choice, no?"

Abu pleaded with the men to let his family proceed. He referred to passages in the Quran that allow Christians to live if they pay the *jizya* (Islamic tax). For ninety agonizing minutes, the discussion continued, as if a bomb were ticking and destined to go off any second. As they talked, an ISIS fighter wielding a sword circled Abu, ready to strike if he tried to run.

"Enough," declared the leader. He grabbed Abu by the arm and led him away as his wife, mother, and sister wept, pleaded, and prayed. "Prepare to die," he said, pushing Abu to his knees. "Last chance. Will you convert to Islam?"

Abu looked back to the three women, then heavenward. He prayed for strength, wisdom, and courage. Even though he felt weak and expected the sword to plunge into him at any moment, he sensed God's peace strengthening him. "No, I will not be a Muslim," he stated. "I do *not* denounce Jesus."

The man raised his sword. Abu bowed his head, closed his eyes, and prayed. Then he heard another vehicle arrive and exhaled. Another black SUV. Out came another ISIS official, who inquired about the situation and then walked over to Abu.

"I have a message for you to deliver to your church leaders as you leave our land," he said. "We are victorious. And we will follow you Christians all over the world. We will reach the Vatican and convert the pope to Islam if we have to."

Abu didn't know what to say but reminded himself not to utter anything disrespectful toward the Muslims. *Simply be honest*, he told himself. "We wish no harm on your people," he said. "Only to practice our faith as we please."

The official looked at him and spit. "Get out of here, you dogs," he said, turning and walking away.

At a second checkpoint, ISIS soldiers again detained the family. They called officials at the first checkpoint and were instructed to check the car for valuables. Abu surrendered all he had. When a guard found money that Abu's wife had hidden beneath a seat, he ordered the family out of the car.

"If you convert," said one guard, "all that we took from you will be given back. You will even be protected. So, tell us you embrace Islam."

"I am a Christian," said Abu.

As before, a long round of verbal volleys ensued. Each time the ISIS guard asked Abu to convert, and each time Abu politely but firmly said he was a Christian and would not.

Finally, another guard—a supervisor—came from the booth and fired questions at Abu. *This man*, Abu thought, *is different from the rest, almost like an actor playing a part but deep down not that character himself.*

"So, you have left behind a home and would be willing to pay the tax?" the supervisor asked.

Abu nodded. Yes, the previous checkpoint had taken substantial money that could be used for the tax. And yes, they did own a house.

The supervisor instructed the interrogating guard to make a call. After the guard left, the supervisor turned to Abu. "Begone," he said. "Fast."

Abu felt like a fish that had been hooked and fighting for its life when suddenly the fisherman cut the line. He nodded his thanks and returned to the car.

Upon reaching Erbil, they saw that the city was already over-populated with Syrian war refugees. Because of the ISIS purge in Iraq, the city was expanding even more each day. What did most of these refugees have in common? They were Christians whose lives had been pulled out from underneath them. Students who had been ready to graduate from the University of Mosul now had no records to show they had even been enrolled. Young people engaged to be married now didn't even know where their fiancées were. Adults who had jobs now were jobless.

They sacrificed it all. They left behind their homes, the lives they had lived, and their hopes for the future, choosing instead to trust in God and serve him wherever he would lead.

The conditions in Erbil were miserable. Nauseating smells rose from garbage and raw sewage. People curled up beneath makeshift tents made of blankets, towels, or scrap materials—anything to protect them from the relentless sun and oppressive heat. They searched desperately for water and food.

Amid all this, Abu set up a lean-to tarp for his family. "Now," he said quietly, "we thank God for a safe journey." And they bowed their heads to pray.

As Abu and his family did, we must remember that the God we serve is with us wherever we go. We must place our hope in him, not in a place or circumstances.

God is far less concerned about where we live than where our hearts are. He cares most about where we place our trust, what we value, and whether the desire of our hearts is to focus our eyes on him. He is pleased when we are so focused on him that we, as the writer of Hebrews did, can affirm our hope and trust with these words: "But as it is, they desire a better country, that is, a heavenly one. Therefore God is not ashamed to be called their God, for he has prepared for them a city" (11:16).

2

The Mother behind Bars

Asia Bibi
Pakistan

Pausing from her work in the fields under the hot sun, Asia took a refreshing drink from the same spigot as the Muslim women. That's when her persecution began.

"Now it is contaminated, you infidel thief," someone blurted out. "Your prophet was born without a father."

"Our Christ sacrificed his life on the cross for our sins," Asia replied. "What has your prophet done for you? Our Christ is alive; your prophet is dead. Our Christ is the true prophet of God, and yours is not true."

Such verbal exchanges ultimately led Asia's coworkers to report her "blasphemous" words to the village's religious leaders, who imprisoned her. At the prison, the authorities told Asia that she could be released: All she had to do was convert to Islam. She refused.

"You can kill me, but I will never leave Jesus," she declared.

Although a group of Christians came to her defense, she was convicted of violating subsection C of Pakistan's 295 blasphemy laws—blasphemy against the prophet Muhammad—and was sentenced to death. Asia's case has drawn international attention calling for abolishment of such laws. Meanwhile, years after Pakistani authorities removed Asia from the field and jailed her, Isha and Isham—her two daughters—wait for their mother to come home.

Two years after the incident, her daughters talked about their mother being taken away because of her stand for Jesus. Still distraught, they shared how much they missed her. "Mama loves us," said Isham. "She would take us to the bazaar, and I would help her with daily work like cleaning or other simple work that I could do. She would help us prepare for school before she went to her job. And sometimes on no-school days we would follow her to the fields after Papa went to his job as a bricklayer."

After Asia was imprisoned, her husband, Ashiq, seldom took the girls with him when he visited her. But because their hearts ached for her, he relented a few months later.

"Oh, my daughters are growing up," Asia said when she saw them.

The two girls longed for a hug, but that could not happen because of the bars between them. So Asia stretched her fingers through the bars in order to feel the fingers of the little girls she had given birth to, prayed for, and for whom she had dreamed big dreams.

"You must leave now," a guard commanded Ashiq.

Isham looked at the guard, then back at her mother. "Come home soon, Mama," she said.

Asia's imprisonment did not stop the persecution of her family and those who supported her. Muslims harassed Ashiq and the children so much that they had to move five times in seventeen months. An imam (Muslim teacher) at a mosque in northwestern Pakistan even issued a fatwa against Asia, offering a six-thousand-dollar reward to anyone who would kill her. The reward was a sizable sum of money for people who lived on just a few dollars a day. Her family worried that a prison guard would try to kill her or that a kitchen worker might poison her food.

Two Pakistani politicians—Governor Salman Taseer and Federal Minister of Minorities Shahbaz Bhatti—spoke out publicly in support of Asia. Bhatti recorded a video in which he stated that he would not be deterred by those who "want to impose their radical philosophy on Pakistan.... I believe in Jesus Christ, who has given his own life for us. I know what is the meaning of the cross.... And I am ready to die for a cause. I am living for my community and suffering people, and I will die to defend their rights."

Soon afterward, he did. So did Taseer. Assassins murdered both of them.

Bhatti's favorite verses were Matthew 5:10–11: "Blessed are those who are persecuted for righteousness' sake, for theirs is the kingdom of heaven. Blessed are you when others revile you and persecute you and utter all kinds of evil against you falsely on my account."

As much as we might try to cling to the things of this world, the faithful lives of these brothers and sisters in Christ remind us that Jesus followers are not of this world. Yet just because our ultimate destination is not of this world doesn't mean we have no responsibilities here on earth. God still calls all of his people to be faithful while on earth—to pray, to know and apply his Word, to be salt and light wherever we live, and to love one another.

Asia, Ashiq, Isha, Isham, the family of Shahbaz Bhatti—and other brothers and sisters in Christ—are being persecuted and incarcerated and are suffering even worse fates for the cause of Christ. They continue to glorify God, knowing and demonstrating to the world that our true hope lies in heaven, in eternity with Jesus. They know that God is faithful and always uses his obedient people to further his work on earth—and that includes bringing good out of their own horrible circumstances. Unified with the global family of Jesus followers around the world, they treasure our prayers for strength and the will to sacrifice everything for Jesus. May they find strength from their brothers and sisters in faith.

3

Hope from on High

Hussein

Iran

By age seventeen, Hussein was a full-fledged drug addict trapped in a prison of his own choices. He was hungry for something more, even though he didn't know what. But he happened upon it while channel surfing one day. A particular television show stood out above the rest. Transmitted by satellite far above Iran, it carried the gospel message straight into Hussein's home.

That day, Hussein heard the message that Jesus died for his sins and wanted a relationship with him. He began to understand that Jesus was about love and compassion, grace and hope, not rules and regulations.

This message of compassion created a deep struggle within him. One part of him related to these statements: *I'm a drug dealer. Drug dealers are bad. So I'm bad. Surely God hates me.*

Yet the man on the television had said the opposite: "God loves you right where you are, whether you are a world ambassador or a drug addict. You matter to him. And he wants you to live the fullest life possible for him."

Those words, and the simple gospel message, penetrated Hussein's hardened heart and mind. He committed his life to Jesus that day, and his life turned from hopeless to hopeful, from lost to saved, from death to life. His desire for drugs faded. His love for other people grew stronger.

And in Iran, the change caused some people to want to kill him and snuff out the hope of Jesus. His Muslim father turned on Hussein, reporting him to authorities in hopes that his "apostate" son would be arrested. His father's response actually understated how much he despised Hussein's decision to follow Jesus. "I hope they decide to hang you [for apostasy]," his father said. "If they do, I will be the one who'll put the rope around your neck."

Hussein was indeed arrested. To honor Hussein's father for his military service during the Iran-Iraq War, the judge chose not to have his son executed. Instead, he was thrown into a prison where guards were free to carry out their own form of justice.

Hussein wanted to stand for Jesus; they broke one of his legs.

Hussein wanted to praise God with music; they broke all his fingers.

Hussein wanted to bow before Christ in humility; they ripped open his back with forty lashes from a whip.

Then Hussein was released.

His high school expelled him, giving him no chance to further his education or attend a university. All his academic records were deleted, as if telling the world, *This person never existed.*

But Hussein not only existed; his time of painful persecution tested his faith and actually taught him to live more fully for God than before the persecution began. Rather than relying on human relationships to sustain him, Hussein placed his ultimate hope in God, who through John communicated these words: "Do not be surprised, brothers, that the world hates you" (1 John 3:13).

Hussein, who simply responded to the message of hope featured on a television broadcast, learned quickly that God wants his people to make him their highest priority, knowing that our love for him will in turn fuel our love for others.

During Hussein's time in prison, his love did grow. With each sacrifice required of him—his leg, his hands, his back, his future—he continued to honor God and told others about him. Despite his suffering, Hussein wrote to some Christians, "None of these punishments made me upset, except that I cannot play music for the Lord now."

His love for Jesus and willingness to forgive spoke most loudly when he shared the gospel with the prison guard in charge of his torture. Deeply touched, the guard gave Hussein his card and asked the teenager to contact him later so he could learn more. What an impact we can have when we rely on God and his Spirit to help us endure the sacrifices of faith and express Christ-centered, compassionate love to those around us.

4

Rising above the Family Beatings

Nadia and Rachel

Pakistan

Whenever eleven-year-old Nadia walked by the neighborhood church, her parents' admonition jolted her from curiosity. Their words waved a finger of warning in her mind: "Nadia, you are to ignore the infidels and their church. It is an affront to your Muslim faith."

Still, as she tugged her colorful headscarf around her head and walked hurriedly past the church, the building itself, the cross that towered above it, the people inside, and the God she could overhear them talking about piqued her interest.

"Jesus," she heard a man say over the church loudspeaker, "is the way, the truth, and the life. " Nadia did not know what these words meant, yet they intrigued her. *If Jesus is the way*, she wondered, *then why am I a Muslim?* Those words proved to be spiritual seeds planted in the deep, rich soil of her soul, and they would bear fruit.

In time, Nadia became friends with a girl about her age, Rachel, who attended the church and lived nearby. This gave Nadia the opportunity to pepper Rachel with all sorts of questions she had stored up during the years.

"Who is this Jesus you speak of?" Nadia asked.

"He is God-become-man, the maker of all."

"Even me?"

"Yes, Nadia, even you," said Rachel. "And me. And everyone. He loves us and desires a relationship with us."

"What does he *expect* of us?" asked Nadia. "What must we do to be in his kingdom? What rules must we keep? What rituals must we perform?"

Rachel touched her friend's hand while lightly shaking her head. "It is not like that. He doesn't want your rituals or your rules. He wants your heart. Your trust. With that, you will *want* to obey."

What kind of God is this? Nadia wondered.

After Rachel gave her a Bible, Nadia discreetly started reading it and began to understand. This was a God of grace. Of love. Of compassion. He even knew the exact number of hairs on her head and would leave ninety-nine sheep to save one—perhaps her. This God was quite unlike the one she was raised to believe in, and she desired to be part of his kingdom.

Soon Nadia prayed to place her trust in Christ, a secret she shared only with Rachel. But when Nadia's brother, Miled, discovered her praying and later going to church, he flew into a rage. He began beating her weekly.

He insisted that she deny Christ.

She refused.

He followed her to church one morning, caught up with her, grabbed her by the back of the neck, took her home, and beat her black and blue.

"How dare you enter that church!" he exclaimed. "Have you forgotten that you are a Muslim? You're never to set foot in that church again!"

"I should be free to attend church," she protested.

He picked up a wooden bowl and slammed it into her forehead, splitting the skin above her eye. As blood poured out, he shoved her into her bedroom and locked the door. He kept her there for weeks, entering only to give her small amounts of food and water but many welts and bruises. Not one of her other family members objected to his brutality or did anything to help her.

Finally, she escaped and found refuge with a pastor and his family. Because Nadia was a former Muslim, however, her presence put others at risk. Fearing retaliation, they soon asked her to find someplace else to live. When she wanted to be baptized, three pastors turned her down because they feared they would be attacked or their churches would be burned. Eventually, a pastor in a distant town agreed to baptize Nadia. She felt a happiness she had never felt before.

God then blessed her with a Christian man, whom she later married. But when her parents learned of the marriage, they registered kidnapping complaints against the man. They claimed he had lured her away from her Muslim faith. Miled found the couple and beat Nadia's husband so badly his eardrum ruptured.

Because the couple had to go into hiding, Nadia's husband could not find work. Other Christians, however, came alongside and helped him start his own business so he could earn money and still keep a low profile.

Beatings. Ostracizing. False accusations. Nadia and her husband have made the sacrifices and endured the abuse in order to cling to their faith in Christ. Christian workers who help this couple marvel at their fortitude and their thankfulness.

During a time of prayer with another Christian, Nadia did not mention her own needs. She said only this: "Oh, Jesus, Son of God, you know me very well. You saved my husband's life when my brother attacked him and beat him badly. When we were hungry, you provided meals and a place to live. Jesus, we trust that you will never leave us. Amen."

Amen indeed. Her hope rests in the confidence that Jesus will never leave us. His great, sacrificial love inspires us to treat others as he has treated us. "'For I was hungry and you gave me food, I was thirsty and you gave me drink, I was a stranger and you welcomed me, I was naked and you clothed me, I was sick and you visited me, I was in prison and you came to me.' … And the King will answer them, 'Truly, I say to you, as you did it to one of the least of these my brothers, you did it to me'" (Matthew 25:35–36, 40).

What a privilege we have to thank God for taking care of us by being his hands and feet to care for others, whether they live next door or in a faraway country. May we pray for God's guidance in discovering their needs and learn to be more sensitive to the Holy Spirit's leading in caring for them.

5

Loving Christ above All

Musa
Somalia

In the village of Yonday, near Kismayo in Somalia, Musa Mohammed Yusuf had many roles. He was husband to Helima, whom he had been in love with seemingly forever. He was father of three cherished sons: Omar, twelve; Ali, eleven; and Salat, seven. A follower of Jesus, Musa was also leader of a house church, whose people he had served honorably for years. Above all, God had called him to share the truth of Jesus in a country on the east African coast where people strongly oppose that truth.

Every role we have in life exacts a price, and some exact a higher price than others. Musa learned this painful truth in July 2009.

Each day when he walked among the villagers, Musa engaged in quiet conversations here and there that he hoped would lead to "Jesus talk." One woman always listened intently. Never coming too close, she was always there on the edge of a group of people. Her face was mostly covered, but her ears obviously took in every word he spoke.

Like most Somali women, she had been tattooed with henna when she was a little girl. Her arms and part of her face were covered with intricate patterns and designs. She was, he knew, married to a high-ranking leader in al-Shabab, an Islamic extremist group in Somalia.

"My prayer is that I will have the opportunity to lead her to Christ," Musa told his friend Ahmed.

Ahmed pursed his lips and shook his head. "Musa, you are my friend, and I honor you for loving God as you do and sharing your faith so freely. But you are playing with fire. You know who her husband is."

"Yes, I know," Musa replied. "And I also know that God's Word tells us to preach the gospel to all nations, including ours. I don't see any exceptions."

"But you could put yourself in danger," said Ahmed. "You could put your family in danger."

"If nobody dares to share Christ with her, then her life, in eternal terms, is more than in danger," Musa stated. "We are not responsible for outcomes, Ahmed, but we are responsible for sharing."

"Even if it could get you killed?"

Musa paused. "Yes, even if it could get me killed."

"But your fam—"

Musa held up a hand. "Ahmed, God is bigger than my family. I love my wife. I love my children. But we are told in the Bible to love Christ above all."

That night, Musa and his wife prayed for that Muslim woman. The next day, when Musa struck up conversations in the marketplace, the woman came near. Musa nodded a greeting to her and then said, "Each day I see you here. Your eyes are inquisitive about this God of whom I speak. Your ears are listening."

She nodded.

"I have a gift for you," he said, glancing left then right.

Her eyes widened. She looked down and saw him slip a small, dark book out from a bag. It was a Bible.

She also glanced furtively from side to side. "Thank you," she whispered, taking the gift. "Thank you so much." Then she quickly left.

A week later, she told Musa that she had found a place in her heart for the Christ of the Bible. "I am committed to following him," she declared, "not Allah."

Musa beamed, not as a reflection of pride in himself, but in honor to God. The next week, however, the woman did not show up. Nor the following week. Musa became worried.

Finally, the woman came, but this time her head was bowed, her eyes were less inquisitive, and the left side of her face was purplish with bruising. Her husband had noticed a change in her and asked why. She told him about her conversion to Christ, and he beat her.

A few days later, a group of Muslim men—henchmen of the woman's husband—showed up at Musa's home and began screaming at him for "converting" the woman. They demanded that Musa tell them where an influential Christian leader named Mberwa could be found. Musa had never heard of him.

"We will give you two days," the militant leader said. "Have Mberwa here when we return … or else."

When the men left, Musa's wife insisted that he leave Somalia. Reluctantly, he traveled to a refugee camp in Kenya. Two days later, while Helima was making lunch for herself and the boys, the henchmen arrived at Musa's home. When they discovered he had left, two men grabbed Omar and Ali, tied their feet together, and blindfolded them. Somehow Helima and Salat escaped and eventually reconnected with Musa in Kenya. But their two older sons would pay the price for what their killers called "the sins of their father." They were beheaded.

That same month, eight other Christians were martyred in Somalia for their faith. A month later, in August, a fourteen-year-old boy who had converted from Islam was shot and killed. In September, a woman was shot and killed because she had six Bibles.

In a world where most people "play it safe" to avoid suffering, many of our devoted Christian brothers and sisters suffer atrocities and die sacrificially because they love Christ above all else. Like Musa and his family, they take to heart Paul's words: "For it has been granted to you that for the sake of Christ you should not only believe in him but also suffer for his sake" (Philippians 1:29).

Jesus followers in communities and countries hostile to Jesus understand suffering for Christ's sake to be a normal part of the Christian life. They willingly choose Christ above all else. They remain fearlessly and sacrificially faithful to the sovereign God they serve.

We can never predict how people will react to what we say or do. We don't know what the consequences will be. But to refuse to live for Christ above all else is to let go of the hand of God and give the enemy control.

What a privilege we have to stand with these brothers and sisters who live out their faith. They are living examples to us of God's mighty power. They demonstrate amazing trust in the God who is faithful to those who serve him.

May we be faithful to pray for courage, guidance, and wisdom. And may we pray for persecuted Jesus followers who can teach us so much about living sacrificially for God.

6

After the Bomb Came the Angels

Khalida
Pakistan

On a September morning, Khalida Marriam, eight months pregnant with a baby boy, went to All Saints Church in the old quarter of Peshawar, Pakistan. As is customary, she left her shoes at the door and went inside to join her fellow believers in worship. No one sitting with her could have anticipated or even imagined the violent acts that soon would change Khalida's life and the lives of many other Jesus followers.

As the crowd of worshippers exited the building, many found their shoes and headed toward the courtyard for a meal. There, two suicide bombers detonated enough explosives to leave more than a hundred people dead. Another 150 were injured. Severed limbs and bloody clothing littered the scene.

It was the deadliest known attack on Pakistani Christians in history. That night many of the world's largest newspapers covered this tragedy, as did television stations, websites, and blogs.

But by the next day, journalists and bloggers had moved on to other news stories.

Khalida will never forget that day. A ball bearing—shrapnel from one of the bombs—ripped through her abdomen, instantly killing her unborn child. She also suffered a broken left arm and multiple fractures in both legs.

At the hospital, the doctor performed a C-section to deliver Khalida's son, who never drew his first breath. The doctor treated her arm and put rods in her legs to help them heal. The care was substandard, however. Two weeks after the bombing, the rods began rusting, endangering her life.

As Khalida cried tears of pain and frustration in the hospital, Christians stepped in and offered financial help to get her moved into a better medical facility. When she heard why they had come, she cried tears of joy.

"When God heals me and I leave the hospital," she said, "my first stop will be at the church to say thanks to God."

Accompanied by her husband and mother, Khalida then bowed in prayer with these supportive Christians. After she was transported to the other hospital, her mother said, "I heard angels are in heaven, but I see angels standing right before me. We never thought about going to this kind of expensive hospital."

When she learned that thousands of brothers and sisters in America were praying for her, Khalida said, "They are all saints. They are all angels."

Some people might argue that Khalida and the others who attended that church are the true saints, the true angels. After all, they courageously worship in a country where many people stridently oppose their faith in Jesus. They put their lives on the line sacrificially in order to worship the one true God.

Even after such terrible attacks, survivors such as Khalida still trust God wholeheartedly. They still place their hope in him. They still praise him. They still thank members of the body of Christ who help them.

"We pray every day to the Lord," Khalida said of her mother, husband, and daughters. "We read the Bible every evening and pray to the Lord for my healing and to bless the people who are helping me."

Jesus followers throughout the world are all indeed blessed to get to know people such as Khalida. To us, they are not "yesterday's news." They are in our minds, hearts, and prayers day and night because they are our sisters and brothers, fathers and mothers in the global family of Jesus.

Paul reminds us that as a body of believers, we are to take on one another's joys and sorrows: "If one member suffers, all suffer together; if one member is honored, all rejoice together" (1 Corinthians 12:26). This is true no matter where we live. No matter how different our life circumstances may be. No matter how great or small our needs may be.

If God's church is truly a worldwide family, then of course we suffer when another Jesus follower is suffering—whether that person lives in our home or many time zones away. Of course we want to extend a helping hand when another Jesus follower is in need. Of course we want to pray for this person as we do for the person across from us in our Bible study group. And of course we rejoice when we see the mighty power of God at work in that person's life.

Pray that God will continue to use the worldwide persecution of Christians to bind us together in a tapestry of Spirit-filled unity so we can truly experience what it means to be members of one body, joint heirs in the family of God.

7

A "Fool" for Christ

Kazim
Pakistan

After eight days of being forced to chop wood from sunrise to sunset, Kazim hardly recognized the ax. Once ash white, its handle was now red from his bleeding hands.

"Now will you cast aside this Christ love?" asked Mohammed Shafiq, a village elder. "Now will you come to your senses?"

Kazim was bent over, exhausted, thinking of his wife, Yasmeen. Sweat dripped from the tip of his nose. His clothes reeked. He shook his head and exclaimed, "No. Never."

"You are a fool," said Shafiq, raising his beating stick high as if he too were chopping wood. His face reflected a blend of satisfaction and frustration. With an audible *oomph*, he slammed the stick across Kazim's well-blistered back.

"Ahhh!" Kazim yelled, grimacing and trying to find the will to withstand yet another blow.

"Quit loafing," the elder said. "We need more wood." Then he swiftly kicked Kazim into the dirt.

Before this persecution began, Kazim farmed by day and evangelized by night. After one of his twelve-hour days, he bicycled home to share a quick meal of chapati and rice with Yasmeen.

"You are wearing yourself thin," she said to him. "You cannot do it all."

He looked at her, the woman whose smile still melted his heart. "The sooner I spread God's Word, the sooner I am back with you," he answered and teasingly took hold of her shawl and pulled her close.

Another day, while Kazim bicycled to the market, Shafiq forced him to stop. "We know you have prayed in the name of Jesus," he said. "Our prophet, Muhammad, is a true prophet. Your prophet is a liar."

"Jesus Christ is the true and living God," Kazim replied. "I worship him and preach his message to other people."

"Is this true?" the elder asked, his eyes squinting. Nodding his head slightly in mock threat, he continued, "Well, let's see what other people think of your worshipping and preaching this Jesus dung."

Shafiq turned to the crowds scurrying from vendor to vendor. "Did you hear this, my friends?" he shouted above the din. "This man—this lower-than-a-snake man—boasts that he bows before Jesus and gloats in telling others of this false God."

Like angry bees, passersby descended on Kazim. Joined by Shafiq, they dragged him away. That's when they forced him to chop wood until he would recant his faith in Christ. When he did not recant, they let him go.

But one night as Kazim prepared for his nightly ministry, Shafiq and five other militant Muslims confronted him again. Kazim beckoned his seven-year-old nephew, Rachid, to come to him. He turned to the boy.

"Today they will kill me," he whispered. "Please take my Bible and keep it with you." He then gently pushed the boy away, as if his nephew were a little boat and Kazim were sending him off to sea.

When Kazim turned his head, Shafiq brandished a semiautomatic pistol and anxiously fingered its trigger. He pointed it at Kazim's head. "Today I will shoot you if you do not accept the prophet Muhammad as the one and only true prophet."

Kazim looked intently into his eyes. "I cannot do this. If you want to shoot me, do it. I will happily accept being killed. But remember; if this is not God's will, you cannot kill me."

Shafiq kept the pistol pointed at Kazim's head for a few minutes. Then his hand began to shake. He pulled out his cell phone and reported to the police that Kazim had tried to rob him.

Later, after Kazim arrived at the police station, officers initiated a new round of torture that lasted for thirteen days.

They tied his hands behind his back.

They beat the bottoms of his feet.

They yanked on his beard, and one officer said, "The prophet Muhammad had a beard, and you dare compare our prophet to Jesus!"

They dragged him across the dirt floor. Mocked him. Spit on him.

Sometimes they stripped off his clothes and lashed his back and buttocks with a leather strap.

"This can all stop when you accept Islam," one man said.

"No."

The officer slapped him across the face, and Kazim shook his head no.

Finally, the police officers registered the false robbery charges against him and sent him to a district jail. Pain radiated through his shoulders and across his back. Weak and too exhausted even to speak, Kazim still felt a peace he could barely comprehend, especially when he held a tattered Bible that a fellow prisoner had given him. His lone frustration? His eyes were too swollen to read that Bible; so the inmate who'd given it to him read to him every day.

Four months after Kazim's arrest, he was released on bail. When he returned home, Yasmeen was gone. Shafiq, his tormentor, had moved in and was using their possessions, claiming their livestock as his own, and reveling in his "ownership" of his new property.

"If you don't leave immediately," he ordered Kazim, "I will shoot you and your wife, when we find her."

With only two dollars to his name, Kazim found Yasmeen in the village. They fled, leaving everything behind. They stopped for help at the houses of various friends, but their friends kept turning them away, fearing that they too would be targets for persecution.

Kazim and Yasmeen fled to another village, where a Christian man allowed them to stay in a small building he owned. He also provided them with clothing, food, and a Bible. "I knew that God would provide help," Kazim said later, "but I didn't know how he would do it. I had one blessing with me—the freedom to preach the Word." Other Christians who learned of their plight stepped in and purchased a rickshaw for Kazim so he could support his family as a taxi driver.

Some people would call Kazim a fool. The scars on his back may never go away. He may never reclaim his home. He may always have nightmares about his beatings.

But Kazim is the kind of fool the apostle Paul wrote about: "We are fools for Christ's sake, but you are wise in Christ. We are weak, but you are strong. You are held in honor, but we in disrepute. To the present hour we hunger and thirst, we are poorly dressed and buffeted and homeless, and we labor, working with our own hands. When reviled, we bless; when persecuted, we endure; when slandered, we entreat. We have become, and are still, like the scum of the world, the refuse of all things" (1 Corinthians 4:10–13).

No amount of earthly humiliation or personal sacrifice can suck the life of Jesus out of a person whose eyes are fixed on him. We may be weak in ourselves, yet we are strong in him. "We forget all our worries," Kazim said recently, "and even today we still feel fresh in Jesus's faith. I start each day in prayer and then drive my rickshaw."

May each of us walk in such faith no matter what comes our way.

Martyrs in History

Dietrich Bonhoeffer
1906–1945
Germany

The Son of God bore our flesh, and for that reason bore the cross. He bore all our sins, and through his bearing brought about reconciliation. Thus are his disciples called to bear.

Dietrich Bonhoeffer, *Meditations on the Cross*

On April 9, 1945, less than a week before Allied troops liberated the Flossenbürg death camp, Nazis hanged Dietrich Bonhoeffer, a Lutheran minister who resisted them during the 1930s and 1940s.

Bonhoeffer grew up as an outstanding student from a middle-class family. He graduated from the University of Berlin and then studied for a year at Union Theological Seminary in New York. In the ghettos of Harlem, he taught Sunday school and led Bible studies and experienced the horrors of racial hatred. By age twenty-five, he was lecturing on systematic theology at the University of Berlin.

When Hitler came to power in 1933, Bonhoeffer emerged as a leading spokesman for the Confessing Church, the center of Protestant resistance to the Nazis. In response to anti-Jewish laws that spring, Bonhoeffer declared in a sermon that the church must oppose the state when it makes biblically wrong judgments. If a mad driver drove a car recklessly and injured people, he reasoned, it wasn't enough just to help the wounded. Rather, other people needed to do everything possible to stop the car. At the time, an increasing number of Christians supported Hitler's National Socialist movement, and most of Bonhoeffer's congregation walked out of the service in disgust.

After the Protestant Church of Germany voted to support Hitler, Bonhoeffer helped launch a breakaway Lutheran group called the Young Reformers. They vowed to be true to God's Word and to oppose Aryan anti-Jewish laws. Later, Bonhoeffer became a leading spokesman for the Confessing Church. His book *Life Together* describes the life of the Christian community in that seminary.

Bonhoeffer's more well-known book, *The Cost of Discipleship*, attacks "cheap grace," which he defined as an excuse for moral laxity. He considered making sacrifices as necessary to the Christian life: "Being expelled, despised, and abandoned by people in one's suffering … is an essential feature of the suffering of the cross, yet one no longer comprehensible to a form of Christian life unable to distinguish between bourgeois and Christian existence."

He described suffering as being about severing our ties to the world. Therefore, it should not be looked on as something Christians should do with a sense of pity, morbidity, or complaint. Sacrifice, yes. But sacrifice with no pity attached.

"The cross is not the horrible end of a pious, happy life, but stands rather at the beginning of community with Jesus Christ," he wrote. "Walking under [the] cross is not misery and despair, but refreshment and peace for one's soul; it is the highest joy."

Bonhoeffer was arrested in 1943 and imprisoned in Berlin. Although his life was spared initially through the intervention of a relative high up in the government, that person was implicated in anti-Nazi plots. On April 8, 1945, Bonhoeffer had just finished conducting a church service in the prison at Schoenberg when two soldiers came in. "Prisoner Bonhoeffer, make ready and come with us," one ordered.

As he left, Bonhoeffer turned to his fellow prisoners. Reflecting the joy of suffering in community with Jesus, he said, "This is the end—but, for me, the beginning—of life."

Part II

COURAGE

Be sober-minded; be watchful. Your adversary the devil prowls around like a roaring lion, seeking someone to devour. Resist him, firm in your faith, knowing that the same kinds of suffering are being experienced by your brotherhood throughout the world. And after you have suffered a little while, the God of all grace, who has called you to his eternal glory in Christ, will himself restore, confirm, strengthen, and establish you.

1 Peter 5:8–10

When we live among people who are resistant to or openly hostile toward the gospel, it is hard—sometimes terrifying—to stand strong and live out our identification as followers of Jesus. But since the earliest Bible times, God has called people to serve him as they faced challenging circumstances. God knows the threats and dangers that lie ahead, and he has a message for those who will serve him faithfully.

After Moses died, Joshua faced an uphill battle in leading the ancient Israelites to fight and possess the Promised Land. God said to him, "Have I not commanded you? Be strong and courageous. Do not be frightened, and do not be dismayed, for the LORD your God is with you wherever you go" (Joshua 1:9).

David, who faced many frightening challenges and overcame great difficulties, shared God's sustaining message in Psalm 27:14: "Wait for the LORD; be strong, and let your heart take courage; wait for the LORD!"

Having courage to move forward in obedience despite obvious perils is not based on human emotion, on getting "pumped up" for the challenge. Courage to stand for Jesus does not come from assessing the risks and strategically balancing benefits against losses. It comes from knowing the risks and moving forward anyway. If we want to stand for Jesus, we cannot let fear paralyze our hearts and cause us to disobey.

Human courage will fail the Jesus follower who shares the gospel in a neighborhood where Islamic militants are in control. Human courage is insufficient to motivate a pastor and his wife to remain in ISIS-controlled territory where they hold clandestine Bible studies in order to help new believers grow in understanding and commitment to Jesus. In contrast to the courage we muster by our own strength, courage to face persecution for our faith is rooted in the knowledge that God is at work in and through us to accomplish his will, even in the midst of violent, life-threatening chaos.

Such courage is nurtured by our trust in God's power and strength to stand against insurmountable odds. It draws confidence from the example and promise of Jesus: "When they deliver you over, do not be anxious how you are to speak or what you are to say, for what you are to say will be given to you in that hour.... And whoever does not take his cross and follow me is not worthy of me" (Matthew 10:19, 38).

Such courage matures through our ongoing commitment to view circumstances in light of God's eternal perspective and to rely on God alone for strength to endure. Such courage leads to bold action despite all risks.

In a world in which even small acts that suggest allegiance to Jesus—asking foreign visitors for a Bible, not responding to the Muslim call to prayer, asking questions of a known Jesus follower—can trigger horrible retribution, courage that is rooted in God's power and faithfulness is essential.

The following stories show Spirit-empowered courage at work in the lives of those who bear the mark "I am n" and gratefully trust God to provide for them moment by moment.

8

The Theology of Pain

Naasir and Hoda
Egypt

A low haze of pollution hung over the sprawling city of Cairo, made even more pungent by cigarette smoke and vehicle exhaust. Amid the hustle and bustle, horns honked. Pushy hawkers preyed on tourists who had come to see the ancient tombs, ornate mosques, and of course the Giza pyramids that rise majestically on the western edge of the city. But Naasir and Hoda, the young married couple who walked toward a housing complex, were not tourists. They focused not on the sights but on at last finding a place to live in a rundown apartment building.

As they passed a group of men, one of them spit at Hoda's feet. He mumbled something about her not having her head covered. Hoda understood his scorn. Whereas most Muslim women cover their heads, most Christian women do not.

The landlord, an older woman, welcomed the thirty-something couple and their nine-year-old son, but she looked skeptically at Hoda. Nevertheless, she told them about the apartment and explained the price and terms. Then she asked a few questions about their rental history, income, and other details.

"Well?" Naasir asked. "Can we have it?"

The woman looked unsure, as if something were bothering her. She glanced quickly at Hoda and then looked away. "Yes," she said with a hint of reluctance. "It is yours if you want it."

"Oh, thank you, thank you," said Naasir.

"We are grateful to you," Hoda added.

Finding a place to live had been difficult for them. Twelve times landowners had kicked the couple out of their apartments after learning they were Christians. Yet Naasir and Hoda remained firm in their commitment to be honest if anyone asked if they were Muslims. Once they had been Muslim, but no longer.

Their relief was short lived, however. As they were leaving, the woman's husband appeared. He looked directly at Hoda and then at his wife.

"You told them, of course," he stated, "that the apartment has already gone to someone else, right?"

"I told them they could have it," she replied.

"What?" he exclaimed and then turned to Hoda. "Where is your hijab?"

Hoda glanced at Naasir and said, "I am ... a Christian."

"Then you do not get the apartment!" the man declared.

"I saw her lack of covering," his wife said, "but we need the money. The place has been empty for six months."

"And we have an agreement," said Naasir hopefully.

"You have nothing!" the man said. "Nothing but disrespect for Islam. Leave. Now!"

"This is not fair," said Naasir. "Just because we don't agree—"

"Leave!" the man repeated. "There are millions of people in Cairo. There are thousands of judges. Not one will side with you."

"Come," said Hoda, "we must go."

In Egypt, the "iron furnace" has grown even hotter for Jesus followers during the last few decades. Radical Islamic theology has rooted itself deeper into society. Muslim extremists have infiltrated government departments. The country's constitution now states that Shariah (Islamic) law must be the basis for all legislation. Attacks against Coptic Orthodox Christians, whose ancestors embraced Christianity during the first centuries after Christ, have increased. But Christian converts from Islam suffer the most, Naasir and Hoda among them. Despite such discrimination, they cling courageously to their faith.

Hoda came to Christ as a young woman. When her family learned of her conversion, her mother locked her in her bedroom. Not for a day. Not for a week. For two years!

She was not allowed to talk or eat with her brothers and sisters because of her "infidel" status. Radio provided her only connection to the outside world and her faith. Although her parents thought she was listening to secular music, she actually tuned in to shortwave Christian programs from Europe. As she listened, she wrote down Bible verses on scraps of paper and then hid them in her clothes or pillow when she wasn't memorizing them.

Eventually, her parents began letting her out for short periods of time; beyond that, they still treated her much like a prisoner. One of Hoda's cousins was a Jesus follower, although few people knew it. Learning of Hoda's predicament, he mentioned his cousin's plight to Naasir, a friend in his tightly knit Christian circle.

Naasir was inspired by Hoda's faith and frustrated by her lack of freedom. After contemplating her situation and praying about it, he determined to rescue her. For two years, he saved money in order to liberate her from her bedroom prison. For two years, he prayed about his plan. Finally, it was time to put it into motion.

With her permission, he asked her parents for Hoda's hand in marriage. Her parents knew little about him, only that he was tall, dark haired, and handsome. They presumed he was a Muslim although they never asked. Deciding this was the perfect solution for ridding their daughter of her "infidel" status, they consented to the marriage.

"Happily ever after" stories are not common among Jesus followers in Egypt, but Naasir and Hoda fell in love, were married, and vowed to do all they could to share their faith in Christ with others.

But the furnace of persecution remained hot.

Muslims often harassed and mocked them. Muslim landlords evicted them when they learned of their Christian faith. The birth of their son was a joyful blessing, yet one that added pressure to find a stable living situation. After a move to yet another apartment, their worn and wobbly furniture fell apart. They had no food. The weather turned cold. They slept on the floor. All of this they did gladly because "we felt God was preparing us to trust us with a ministry," Naasir said.

Despite the uncertainties of their life in Egypt, they remain faithful to their calling. Naasir is an evangelist who teaches others how to share God's Word. Hoda spearheads a ministry to shelter women in Cairo who have been evicted from their homes after converting to Christianity. Thankfully, other Christians have helped them find a permanent living situation.

"We have had many chances to leave Egypt," Hoda said, "but we are convinced that we have to be in Egypt to complete our ministry here."

In addition to the ever-present threat of being found out by authorities, they still experience friction with their Muslim families. Now that their son attends school, they face a new and difficult challenge. Every day he encounters resistance to the Jesus-based life and faith he experiences at home.

"He is confused because he hears something in the school and different things in the house," said Naasir. "In school, they teach him that Christians are infidels and even to curse Christ. At home we try to correct this."

Despite serious opposition, Naasir and Hoda courageously embody Mark 8:35: "For whoever desires to save his life will lose it, but whoever loses his life for My sake and the gospel's will save it" (NKJV). They are reminded constantly that the Word of God never promises "happily ever after" endings—just strength and wisdom from God for whatever comes their way. We can learn so much from them.

"In Egypt, our theology is the theology of pain," Naasir explained. "We don't know the theology of prosperity, but we know Jesus."

They know that hope, contentment, and peace can be found only in Jesus. So instead of spending their lives trying to construct a "happily ever after" scenario for themselves, they have the courage to trust God for whatever lies ahead. They are committed to do his will, not their own.

9

From Persecutor to Persecuted

Abdulmasi
Nigeria

After bombing a church, Abdulmasi liked to return to relish his work. To learn the body count. To bask in the glory of killing Christians. This was, after all, a major focus of the fanatical group Jama'atu Nasril Islam in which he participated.

Decades ago, his comrades began calling him "Mr. Insecticide." He earned this nickname because he was, as he explained, "the only one who could organize the killing of insects—the killing of Christians. When you were looking for someone to get rid of insects, then call me. This was my life."

Whenever Muslims in northern Nigeria felt Christians were encroaching, they would call him. He specialized in car bombs, riot planning, and infiltrating Christian organizations, the last of which proved to be his undoing—or, from a biblical perspective, his redemption.

Abdulmasi had known no other life than absolute adherence to Islam. At age five, his family forced him into *almajiri*, an antiquated

Islamic practice popular in West Africa. Muslim families send their young sons away to a local imam. A boy doing *almajiri* might join forty or fifty other young boys in the imam's instruction. Their days are as rigid as those of prisoners.

In the morning, the boys recite the Quran in Arabic, a language they do not understand. They recite it for hours, and literally for years, until they memorize the Quran. The task is not unlike an English-speaking child memorizing the Bible in Chinese.

At midday, the boys walk the streets and beg for food, which they share first with the imam. Afterward, they might study the Hadith, a collection of sayings ascribed to the prophet Muhammad, written by Islamic scholars beginning in the ninth century. In fundamentalist Islamic sectors around the world, the Hadith is the source from which young boys learn the concepts of jihad, paradise, and killing enemies of Allah.

Having lived on a steady diet of this for a decade, Abdulmasi said, "Islam is a teaching of hatred, hatred and nothing more than hatred." And, "If there is any evil in society, they will relate it as a result of Christians." His only solace in this life? A promise of "paradise" if he would kill enemies of Allah.

At age seventeen, wanting desperately to escape a life he hated, Abdulmasi became involved in his first jihad against Christians in the city of Bauchi, Nigeria. The jihadists did not touch women or children, but they did beat and slash men. During this attack, Abdulmasi spotted a man known to be a Christian coming out of his home.

"I began beating his legs so he couldn't run away," recalled Abdulmasi. "He fell down and my boys attacked him, trying to kill him. A seven-year-old boy was the one who slaughtered the man with a knife. Pressing down on his neck, he cut the man. They called the boy 'Chief Slaughterer.'"

After the killing, Abdulmasi rejoiced. "You see, when you do this, when you kill a mosquito," he said, clapping his hands together, "you have achieved something. You smile even though you see blood on your hands. I have gotten rid of the enemy of God, my enemy too."

Years passed. The killings continued. One day Abdulmasi returned to a church he had just bombed only to find something odd happening. Church members who had survived the attack were singing songs.

This infuriated Abdulmasi. When he returned to the mosque, he lamented what he had seen. "They are rejoicing." He huffed. "They are happier." *Why couldn't I rid these mosquitoes from the church?* he wondered.

In frustration, he decided to use a new tactic. He would infiltrate the church as an impostor and look for ways to kill Jesus followers. The next day, he went to the church and told the pastor, "I'm a Muslim, but I want to become a Christian."

The pastor and his congregation eagerly embraced him. "The love I was shown," he later said, "surprised me."

He began attending services regularly. He joined the young adult group, went to baptism class, and was baptized. All the while, he was secretly returning to the mosque to pray and fast.

For six years, Abdulmasi lived this double life. He might bomb a church across town one day and lead a Bible study the next. He was even appointed the young adult leader. But when the church planned a conference and invited a prominent pastor to talk, Abdulmasi was furious. *Why not me? Am I not the young adult leader? Why wasn't I asked to speak?*

He attended the conference, anger churning inside. He specifically prayed that the speaker would fail and that he would be asked to take over. But God had a different plan for Abdulmasi. During the last day of the conference, the pastor spoke on 1 Kings 18, Elijah's challenge to the prophets of Baal.

"How long are you going to waver between two opinions?" the pastor thundered. "If God is God, worship him. If Baal is god, worship him."

Abdulmasi perked up.

"Who are you deceiving?" the pastor continued. "How long now since that day you said you have accepted Christ and you have not been serious? Why are you playing this double game?"

Abdulmasi squirmed inside. *This man knows about me! Who told him? Soon he will call out my name.*

"Just humble yourself," the pastor continued. "Just stand up. Let me pray for you, and the Lord will forgive you for all you have been doing. Forget that you are an armed robber. Forget that you are a killer. Forget all those things. Stand up!"

Abdulmasi stood up. His double life ended. When he went forward to profess his faith in Christ—this time for real—he began a new life in God's grace. He also opened himself up to retribution from the jihadists with whom he had previously aligned.

"Don't go near the mosque," one of his "boys" later warned him. "They will kill you."

Meanwhile, the church elders were delighted to hear of his commitment but stunned at the revelation of his double life. "What do we do with this man?" they debated. "Oust him? Embrace him?" They prayed for three days.

Their decision? They would hide him to save his life. "My son," the pastor told Abdulmasi, "God is going to use you mightily."

And God has used him. While hiding at the home of another pastor, Abdulmasi could not help but share his faith with Muslims. He always looked for opportunities to introduce Muslims to Christ—and always looked over his shoulder.

Many men credit him with introducing them to Christ. He secretly counseled teachers of the Quran. He built bridges to persecutors of Christians.

Months became years. Years became decades. Abdulmasi married. He and his wife had children. But his jihadist past would not be forgotten. He was still a marked man. On one occasion, when Muslims surrounded his house, he narrowly escaped death by slipping out a back way. Three years later, Muslims confronted his college-age son.

"We have not come to rob you," one said. "We have come to kill you because you are your father's son." And they slit his throat.

"It was very difficult," said Abdulmasi, "but there is no sacrifice that is too big for God." And no hurt too deep that God's grace cannot cover.

Demonstrating great courage, Abdulmasi reached out to share Christ with the man who had helped plan his son's death. The man rebuffed Abdulmasi; however, the man's son heard about what happened and showed up at Abdulmasi's house.

"Please," he said, "tell me about your Christ."

It is never too late for God to redeem us. Looking back at a life in which he persecuted Christians, lived a double life, and then was persecuted himself, Abdulmasi can only shake his head. "If you want to win Muslims," he said, "you have to love them, not with the human type of love, but the love you, yourself, have experienced through Christ. People are seeing me share my real heart now. If it were not for the grace of God, I would not be who I am."

The change in Abdulmasi from persecutor to persecuted reflects a step of courage that makes a powerful impact. As the apostle Paul wrote in Galatians 1:23–24, "They only were hearing it said, 'He who used to persecute us is now preaching the faith he once tried to destroy.' And they glorified God because of me."

It is never too late for any of us to run into God's arms. Pray that others who have known nothing but a life of hatred will be introduced to the God of love and forgiveness. Pray that they, like Abdulmasi, will have the courage to embrace Christ and leave the killing behind.

10

Swimming against the Current

Yousef
Middle East

Yousef opened the bottle of pills. There were plenty to do the job. But before he did it, he felt obliged to do at least a cursory review of the twenty-plus years he'd lived. When he started mentally rewinding those years, they unraveled in a litany of failure after failure, disappointment after disappointment, defeat after defeat. He quickly wrote off that idea.

Yousef had tried so hard to do everything right. He attended mosque. He recited his daily Quranic prayers. But by the time he was seventeen, Yousef had walled himself off from family and would-be friends. An emptiness starved his heart, and though he tried to fill it with everything from drugs to alcohol to gangs, nothing worked. That was why he started thinking about overdosing on pills.

Then, out of seemingly nowhere, the pleasant face of his grandfather materialized. His memories of the man were not extensive. He rarely saw his grandfather because Yousef lived in the Middle

East and his grandfather had moved to the United States. But the thought of the man brought a smile to his face and a little hope to his heart.

Yousef remembered that his grandfather was a Christian, not a Muslim. And he remembered the time he told him the "salmon story." When he was just a little boy, Yousef had climbed into his grandfather's lap while the man was watching television. The program was showing a scene of salmon swimming against the rapids of a stream.

"Yousef," he said to his grandson, "Christians are like those fish—always swimming against the current, against the world. The ways of the world are always against the ways of Christ. But although they may struggle, the fish that swim against the current are full of life. And those that swim easily downstream with the current, with the world: those fish are dead."

Remembering the story touched something deep within Yousef. He snapped the cap back onto the pill bottle. *I'm on the brink of suicide*, he thought. *What do I have to lose by praying to this God of my grandfather?*

Yousef had no idea how to pray, so he was as honest and down to earth as he could be. "I will not kill myself if Jesus will make everything right in my life." Punctuating it with even more forthrightness, he added, "By the end of tomorrow."

He then fell asleep.

In the morning, he awoke to find his uncle Ishaq sitting on the foot of his bed. "God has laid on my heart that I should come visit you today," he said. "I need to tell you about myself, about how I am truly the son of my father, your now-gone grandfather."

"What do you mean?" asked Yousef.

"Long ago, I determined that the way to be happy was to be rich and powerful and important," he said. "So I thought I would achieve that by becoming a drug smuggler. But then I discovered a new way. A way to be content in all things. I discovered Jesus."

The word *Jesus* jolted Yousef, but his look of surprise morphed into curiosity. "Like grandfather?" he said, leaning forward.

"Exactly," said his uncle. "When I was young, I thought he was a crazy man. Jesus? Really? But when I hit the wall, it was my father, his life and contentment, that I came back to. So we began to talk."

"Like you and I are doing now."

"Indeed."

His story captivated Yousef, who began visiting his uncle regularly to talk about this Jesus. His uncle gave him a Bible, and Yousef was careful when bringing it home. His mother, a leader at the local mosque, hated Christians with a passion. Once, she had ripped a cross pendant from the neck of his uncle's wife and spit in her face.

One day, Yousef simply spoke to God: "Jesus, I ask you into my heart. I lay my sins before you. I long to start over with you."

Then it happened. Yousef's mother found his Bible underneath his bed. Although he was quite a bit taller than she was, she grabbed him by the shirt collar, her face creased in rage.

"Allahu akbar!" ["God is great!"] she screamed, then grabbed a garden hose and started whipping her son. He could not sleep for five days afterward because of the welts on his back.

"The Bible," she told him, "is a dirty book, and Christians are devils." A few days later, she threatened to slit his throat with a kitchen knife.

Yousef wanted to lead his family to the same joy in Christ he had found, but he worried that the attempt could cost him his life. Nevertheless, he carefully talked to others about his faith. Once, he and his older brother were on their knees in prayer when their mother barged into his brother's room. She hit Yousef's head with an iron skillet. She beat his brother and then started to choke Yousef until he nearly lost consciousness.

Another time, Yousef's father threatened to push him off a third-story balcony.

"He told me if he pushed me off, he'd go to jail, my mother would go insane, and my brother would become a beggar on the street," said Yousef. "But he said if I jumped, then everyone would just say my father had a crazy son."

Yousef considered his options with Romans 12:18 in mind: "If possible, so far as it depends on you, live peaceably with all." He decided to jump, in order to avoid bringing dishonor to his family. He survived with only an injured shoulder and a cut above one eye.

"Why did you jump?" his father asked him at the hospital. "I was just trying to scare you so you would return to our faith."

Yousef did not return to his parents' faith. While God doesn't wish for any family to be in discord, he makes it clear that we are to place our relationship with him above all others. Jesus said that for those who follow him, there is the risk that "they will be divided, father against son and son against father" (Luke 12:53).

When our family members don't share our faith, it is vital that they see Christ working in and through us. Consider, if you will, the gentle spirits of Yousef's grandfather and uncle. They captured his heart, not with threats, but with stories that led Yousef in finding the Lord.

Today Yousef chooses to swim upstream just as his grandfather and uncle showed him. He spends much of his time ministering to young Muslims. He helps smuggle Bibles and other Christian literature, and he uses the Internet to help lead young Arabs to Christ.

It's a courageous move. The resistance is great. Each day there is a chance that he will be caught and persecuted. But he swims upstream anyway, knowing he will one day be reunited with his grandfather. His story is a reminder to all followers of Jesus to notice where we are in the stream—whether we are giving our all to keep moving upstream or whether we are floating downstream.

11

Courage to Keep Walking

Sajid
Pakistan

Hours had passed since Sajid, a twenty-seven-year-old evangelist, had boarded a bus in order to share the gospel in one of Pakistan's more dangerous areas. As the bus rumbled along, he conversed with several passengers seated near him. Despite the fact that Muslim extremists in this area prowled for Jesus followers like lions seeking prey, he began talking about Jesus.

What gave him the courage to speak so openly? When he attended Bible school years earlier, Sajid had dreamed that a large open door stood at the entrance to one of Pakistan's prominent cities. He believed the dream was God's way of guiding him in opening new doors for the gospel. During the decade following that dream, Sajid led hundreds of Pakistanis to Christ.

A bearded man seated nearby shook his head. "You Christians do not consider anything about our prophet, so why should we listen to you talk about your Bible?"

Sajid measured his response and resisted any attempt to be impolite. But as 1 Peter 3:15 says, he was prepared to defend the reason for his faith. "Our Bible," he answered, "makes no reference to your prophet."

"The prophet was written in your Bible!" the man retorted angrily. "But you people would not accept it. You changed the words to your own!"

Realizing it would be futile to try to reason with him, Sajid ended the conversation.

Shortly after Sajid got off the bus, about a dozen men grabbed him, tied a blindfold over his eyes, and shoved him into the backseat of a car. Twenty-five minutes later, they dumped him at a compound where other people began questioning him.

"Who are you?" the leader demanded. "Are you a preacher? Are you converting Muslims? Which organization do you belong to?"

Sajid fell silent with fear.

"Are you mute?" another asked. "We will kill you if you don't answer our questions."

"I am telling you the truth," Sajid said. "I am God's preacher."

"If you want us to spare your life, you must deny your faith and become a Muslim. If you don't do as we say, we will torture you. Within thirty minutes, your passion for Christianity will blow away like dust in the wind."

"I am ready for whatever you choose to do to me," Sajid declared. "I am prepared to die for Jesus. I will not lose my passion for him no matter what you do to me."

Sajid's kidnappers strapped him to a tree, tied his hands behind him, and forced him to stand barefoot on a block of ice. While the

Pakistani heat bore down on him, baking the rest of his body, his feet seethed in pain—as if he were standing on a million pins.

Half an hour became an hour. An hour became two hours. Two hours became four. The bottoms and lower sides of Sajid's feet swelled into blisters, tinted in green. He wept but did not speak. Sweat poured from his body, staining his clothes.

"Look," jeered one of the many onlookers. "It is a hundred degrees and the Jesus lover has frostbite!" The crowd laughed.

"Maybe now you will give up this futile running after Jesus and return to where you belong," a tormentor said. "Maybe now you will return to Allah."

Sajid shook his head.

"Then you will be following Jesus on stumps!" the man replied. "When your feet crumble, we will ice down your nubs. When your nubs freeze, we will saw them off. Jesus will turn and look for you, but you will not be there because you will be a man with no legs! Ha! But if you follow Allah, you will not only walk but also run. Isn't that the better option?"

Again, Sajid shook his head.

"Jesus," he cried out, after hours of ice torture. "Help me. Help me, Jesus!"

Sajid later recalled what happened next: "Suddenly, I saw a vision of a radiant angel appearing in front of me. Jesus was with me, like the fourth man when Shadrach, Meshach, and Abednego were in the fiery furnace."

His pain eased. He gained strength. To the surprise of his tormentors and the crowd mocking him, he began singing worship songs. Then he blacked out.

Sajid awoke in the middle of the night lying in a drainage ditch alongside a dirt road. His wallet and a Hebrew language book he'd been carrying sat beside him. A passerby, a modern-day Good Samaritan, checked him in to a local hotel and paid for him to stay there for three days while he recovered. Afterward, Sajid's brother took him for medical treatment and then home to rest.

Jesus never promised a life of ease on earth to those who serve him. But he did promise that he would not abandon us to labor and suffer alone. When he sent his disciples out into the world to spread the truth, as Sajid was doing, Jesus promised, "And behold, I am with you always, to the end of the age" (Matthew 28:20).

The very presence of Jesus with us in the midst of our suffering gives us courage to press on when our own strength fails us. Let's join others—people like Sajid—in God's global family to serve Jesus with our eyes set firmly on him. Let's pray that we will not be deterred from courageous living for God. Let's encourage one another in single-mindedness to keep running after God despite the world's attempts to knock our feet out from under us.

Sajid's tormentors stated that without feet Sajid would be unable to follow Jesus, yet today he is still walking—and still talking—about his beloved Savior.

12

Released to Tell Others

Sara
Iran

As a teenager, Sara was an Islamist prayer warrior, a *Basiji*—a member of a grass-roots Islamic volunteer group that answered to the Iranian Revolutionary Guards. When she prayed in school, all the other girls always expected her to lead them. She fasted so long one time that she wound up in the hospital. To show her devotion to Islam during services, she and her friends would practice self-flagellation. Sara always had more bruises than anyone else, yet her deep spiritual needs remained unfulfilled. She found herself asking questions.

Why am I spiritually empty?

Why do I feel no personal connection to the god of Islam?

Why, during my prayer rituals, do I do everything right and still feel so terribly wrong?

"As a young girl," she recalled, "I asked my mom and dad if I could learn how to pray the Muslim prayers. I would lay out my white prayer cloth on the floor, then place another cloth on top, then lay a handkerchief with a stone—a tablet of compressed dirt from Mecca. We have to put our nose on the stone. After I would finish praying, I would pick up the stone and the handkerchief and underneath would be money. But I didn't want the money. I wanted the truth."

A movie about the life of Jesus changed everything.

Shortly before Sara was to enter the university, one of her sisters returned to their small town from college. She brought a movie about the life of Jesus and dared to share it with Sara.

Sara went into a room away from her family and put the movie into the video player.

"I watched how Jesus loved people," she said later. "I began to cry. At the end of the film, there is a prayer of repentance. I prayed it six times." She rewound the tape to the prayer again and again— backward, forward, backward, forward. "I don't think I realized what repentance meant, but I wanted to be near God."

She fell to her knees and raised her hands. "I was jealous of my sister since she came from college, because she would kneel down and without any Muslim beads, cloth, or stone would lift up her hands and start praying. I wanted to pray and feel close to God like she did."

"God," Sara would pray, "I want to have a connection. With you."

She kept praying. She cried and prayed, asking God over and over for just that—a connection. She wondered, *Could this be what I am looking for?* She wasn't sure.

"Then I began to pray that I would be delivered from sin," she remembered. "That day it was like God was talking to me, through me. He was saying, 'This is the truth. I am the true God. I am the one God.'"

Sara raced into the kitchen to find her sister and tell her the news. Jesus had saved her!

When Sara began praying, it was as if she were learning to talk for the first time. "I had no Bible," she recalled. "I knew hardly anything about Jesus. All I had was a colored picture of Jesus about six inches high with a frame painted with flowers. He was looking to one side. To feel close to him, I would sit on the side where he was looking in the picture. This way, I felt that he was always looking at me."

She began meeting secretly with members of a house church and was given a New Testament. "I was so happy," she said. When Iran became an Islamic republic in 1979, the Bible Society closed. So Christians or curious Muslims often had to travel hundreds of miles to find one.

The house church met in a tiny room with mud walls. "But from those walls," she said, "love came out." They talked about how they engaged with God without being caught. A young man spoke about how he would sit in the family car at night to read Scripture by flashlight. Sara shared her longing to tell others about Christ. But how would she do it?

Sara liked her life. She liked serving Christ. She just needed to find a way to tell others about him. She found a way during her commute to and from work.

"On the bus in the morning on my way to work and in the evening on my way home, I would witness to two or three people," she explained. "In the middle of the bus is a big, long rail dividing the men from the women. I would be on one side witnessing to a woman, but the men across the rail would be listening. They would be very interested."

Sara is well aware of the risk. Being a nominal Christian in Iran is one thing, but evangelizing is another—an invitation for persecution. Still, Sara said, "I can't *not* share Christ with others. I must tell them what released me from spiritual bondage."

Sara knows that finding Christ happened because her sister dared to share with her. So she knows how important it is to tell others about the good news. She courageously follows in the steps of the apostle Paul, who wrote, "Continue steadfastly in prayer, being watchful in it with thanksgiving. At the same time, pray also for us, that God may open to us a door for the word, to declare the mystery of Christ, on account of which I am in prison—that I may make it clear, which is how I ought to speak" (Colossians 4:2–4).

Wherever we go, we take Jesus with us. In what we say. In how we act. In how we pray. May we be courageous in sharing him with others. May we be faithful in praying for courage for our fellow believers.

13

A Most Unlikely Change

Samrita
Malaysia

Whack!

Her father's backhand caught Samrita on the cheek and sent her flailing to the ground. Again. Her nose began to bleed.

"You are worthless to me, Samrita," he said in a Malaysian dialect slurred by drink. "You are worthless to everyone. Like your twelve brothers and sisters."

It was the mid-1990s, and her family was imploding—splintered by fists, alcohol, and words that cut like knives. Her father drank. Her mother cowered in fear, refusing to intervene. And who could blame her? Samrita tried to keep the peace, tried to hold her family together.

"Papa, you don't know what you're saying," said Samrita after he hit her another time. "You don't mean that."

"Oh, poor Samrita," he mocked, "but I *do*." He laughed, shoved a chair at her that bruised her knee, then staggered away to sleep off his night at the bar.

At age eighteen, Samrita started seeing a young Muslim man named Uda. She viewed him as a way out of her father's house, and they married in 1999. Samrita embraced Islam in order to marry, but things did not go well for her. Uda slipped into using drugs and beating her up just as her father had.

"It is as if I am jinxed," she told her friend Aisha.

"You must be more diligent in your devotion to Islam," Aisha replied.

So Samrita began praying five times a day, dressed modestly, recited the Quran, and even planned a pilgrimage to Mecca. But none of these gave her the inner peace she so desperately sought.

Then one day in 2006, a most unlikely change happened. It began with a visit from her father.

Seeing her father jolted Samrita. She opened the door gingerly, warily, fearful memories of her past searing her soul. It had been a long time since she had last seen him.

"What do you want?" she asked in a staccato burst of skepticism.

"Only to say one thing to you."

"And what is that?" she asked.

His eyes glistened. Samrita had never seen this look before. Something had changed.

"I am sorry," he stated.

"Papa?"

"I am not worthy to be your father."

Samrita swallowed hard, then asked, "What has happened to you?"

"I am not the man you knew years ago," he said. "I am a changed man."

Her idealism encouraged her to believe him; her memory encouraged her to doubt. "And how do I know this?"

He held out a small box. "For you."

She opened it. Inside was a necklace with a small wooden cross.

"Samrita," he said. "I have left my anger, my ego, and my stupidity at the foot of the cross. I am now a Christian."

She did not know exactly what this meant. But every month whenever she visited her family after that time, she discovered he had indeed changed. He told all of his children about what Christ had done in his life and begged their forgiveness.

Although her father's words intrigued Samrita, his actions convinced her that whoever this Christ was, he had power.

Formerly a bully, her father was now gentle. Once belligerent, he was now kind. At one time selfish, he was now selfless.

She began asking about this Jesus, and at a Christian seminar in 2008, she accepted Jesus as her Lord and Savior. She did not tell Uda, however. She had found the peace she had longed for and didn't want to spoil it.

When Uda found her Bible one day, he lashed out. He cursed her and kicked her out of the house. Samrita grabbed their two children, ten-year-old Lili and five-year-old Faiz, and took them with her.

Uda decided to divorce Samrita, and he also reported her to the Shariah police in charge of administering Islamic law. They ordered her to appear in court before the religious authorities.

Her fellow believers began to fast and pray, asking for God's favor in Samrita's case. If Uda told the court she had left Islam, Samrita could be sentenced to three years in a walled detention center, euphemistically called a "purification center." There, Muslims would try to convert her back to Islam. If she refused to go to the center, she would face prison.

During the trial, the judge repeatedly asked Uda why he wanted a divorce. Strangely, he refused to answer, even though doing so would have likely meant a prison sentence for the wife who he felt betrayed him by rejecting Islam. The judge granted the divorce, awarding the two children to Uda with no visitation rights for Samrita. But she would not go to prison.

Samrita now attends a Malaysian church with sixty members. She and her father are closer than ever. His love of Jesus became *their* love of Jesus. She has forgiven her father and Uda for abusing her.

Although Uda allows Samrita to visit the children, he has warned her not to share her faith with them. Despite the risk of losing all contact with them, she has the courage to do it anyway.

"With help from the Lord, I will have the right to take care of my kids," she said. Meanwhile, she lives with the confidence that nothing is beyond God's power. She has seen that Christ indeed makes all things new, as 2 Corinthians 5:17 promises: "Therefore, if anyone is in Christ, he is a new creation. The old has passed away; behold, the new has come." She is reminded of this wonderful truth each time she puts on the wooden cross her father gave her. It gives her courage to trust her future to Jesus.

14

Not Welcome Here

Afrooz

Iran

Afrooz, an Iranian Muslim, was not looking for Jesus when she found him.

She was looking for help. For peace of mind. For something to ease her pain.

Her life had unraveled under the stress of work, school, and nagging doubts about her Islamic faith. *Perhaps*, she thought, *I should just leave the stress behind and become a poet.* Poets are highly esteemed in Iranian culture, and this would be far better for her blood pressure.

She cried out to Allah when feeling overwhelmed by life. No, she admitted later, she did more than that. She *threatened*. "If you are going to help me," she prayed, "tonight you should show yourself to me. If you don't show me a sign tonight, I will turn to this material life and be a sinner."

Then she fell asleep and had a vision: "The room was full of light. I thought it was morning, but later I realized it was midnight. I lifted my head and was seeing Jesus Christ. He was wearing white.

Although I had never seen a picture of the Messiah, I recognized that this could be no one else."

She pulled out a pen and paper to take notes if he spoke, and he did, saying, "Come to me, all you who labor and are heavy laden, and I will give you rest."

Then the vision ended. This angered her. She had no context whatsoever for the words he spoke. "I was looking for Muhammad's god," she recalled, "and Jesus the Messiah comes to me! What is this? So I closed up the prayer mat and said, 'I am done with this! I am going to sleep!'"

The next night she again saw the Messiah in a vision. "Didn't I tell you to come under my shadow and come with me and be safe?" he asked her.

Now she was truly perplexed. When the vision ended, she thought, *This is the Messiah coming to me? Is this the real God? I should be seeing Allah or Muhammad.*

At Afrooz's office job, a coworker noted that she seemed out of sorts. She lied, telling him that she hadn't seen her mother in America for some time and that it was bothering her.

Suddenly, the young man blurted out that he followed Jesus and said, "God is always with you. God is love. Bring your complaints to him."

She was stunned. "Usually in Iran," she reflected later, "people working in a company don't come up and say, 'I'm a Christian.'"

So Afrooz showed him the words that had come to her. He discreetly opened his Bible—she had never seen one before—and pointed to Matthew 11:28. She was amazed as she read, "Come to me, all who labor and are heavy laden, and I will give you rest."

"That," she revealed later, "was the beginning of my faith." It also initiated resistance from people who opposed her newfound faith.

When she left to seek another job, she learned that companies working with the Iranian government did not want to hire Christians. "They are under pressure to take out the Christians' benefits, lower their salaries, and offer no insurance," she said. Private companies offered to hire her, but for less money than they would normally offer and with no benefits.

Through her church, she met a Jesus-following man and married him. This triggered the wrath of the Iranian secret police. When the couple arrived at the hotel on their wedding night, they were detained and asked about their church involvement. About their pastor. About proof that they were really married.

Eventually, the police let them go, but the episode so chilled them that they moved to northern Iran, where they hoped to have more freedom to serve Christ. Both became involved in ministries. Afrooz specialized in working with Christian women in Iran and other countries.

When their daughter was born, they were harassed by officials because they chose a Christian name, Emmanuel, for her. After the little girl started preschool, school administrators refused to certify her attendance or provide the necessary documents so she could advance to elementary school. Afrooz worried that the government would take their daughter away from them, saying that she and her husband were not providing a proper education.

Again the family moved on, very much aware of Jesus's words, "Truly, I say to you, there is no one who has left house or wife or brothers or parents or children, for the sake of the kingdom of God, who will not receive many times more in this time, and in the age to come eternal life" (Luke 18:29–30).

It takes courage to face earthly injustice and rest in the hope of Jesus, who promises to sustain his people wherever they are. Individually or together, Afrooz and her family have been shunned wherever they go: workplace, school, hotel, new city. When people treat them unjustly, they do not retaliate with eye-for-eye justice because they know "this isn't all there is." They know there's more to come, in eternity.

Their nomadic, alienated existence brings to mind the passage in the book of Hebrews that says Jesus followers are "strangers and exiles on the earth.… But as it is, they desire a better country, that is, a heavenly one. Therefore God is not ashamed to be called their God, for he has prepared for them a city" (11:13, 16).

Pray for peace of mind for our persecuted brothers and sisters in Christ who step forward in courage every day to stand firm in their faith.

15

Just Giving Out Bibles

Boutros
Syria

It was always dark in the village after sunset. Boutros was in the region where the apostle Paul experienced his life-changing encounter with Jesus Christ on his way to persecute Christians. It had no electricity. This night seemed even darker than most.

Boutros had not returned home for the 4:00 p.m. curfew that had been imposed in the village. It was unsafe for anyone to be on the streets, especially a man who handed out Bibles and talked with Syrians about Jesus. He was easy prey for Muslim extremists, who decried anything or anyone opposing Islam or Muhammad.

"Boutros," a church leader said to him days earlier, "you must stop this, at least for now. We cannot afford to lose you. It is too dangerous."

"But this is what I'm called to do," he replied. "To spread the good news of Christ to the thirsty Syrians."

"Yes, but there is kidnapping and torturing," the church leader countered. "The extremists are cutting Christians into pieces."

Boutros would not stop sharing Jesus.

As the evening deepened, church leaders and others who shared his ministry vision began thinking the worst. People gathered to pray for their friend. Calls to Boutros's cell phone triggered no response. They had no way of knowing his phone had been turned off.

"The image that came to mind," said one friend, "was that Boutros, like the others, had been cut to pieces."

At 9:00 p.m., they were so desperate to learn about their friend that they even called the city's secret police to see if they had arrested him.

"Why was he out on the streets?" they asked.

"Giving out Bibles," they replied.

"Why was he doing that?" the policeman asked. "Is he crazy?"

After the secret police claimed to know nothing about Boutros's whereabouts, his friends became even more concerned. "It was a dark moment for us," recalled a friend who was among those praying. People cried and prayed. "Lord," someone prayed, "he is in your hands. Keep him safe. Protect him."

Morning came. No Boutros.

A full day passed. No Boutros.

Two days passed. No Boutros.

Finally, the entire congregation gathered in the church, so spent they did not even have the energy to eat.

A sudden noise at the door froze them in fear. It swung open. In walked Boutros. The congregation enveloped him in tear-stained hugs.

Tired, unshaven, and dirty, he told his story about being picked up by the secret police.

"Get out of here," an officer had told him, "or we will take you away and you will be gone."

Boutros left that street but not the area. He simply walked one street over and began visiting shop after shop to share Christ's good news. He knew that being salt and light for Jesus required action, not quitting when people opposed his plans.

The police followed him, pulled a black bag over his head, and whisked him away to a prison cell crowded with long-bearded Muslim extremists who had run afoul of the secret police.

"Why are you here?" one asked.

"For sharing the love of Christ," he replied, "which I'd like to share with you too."

And that is exactly what he did.

The next day, the head of the secret police sat across from Boutros and angrily interrogated him.

Boutros responded with love, not like-minded anger. "I was just giving out Bibles," he said. "The Bible teaches us to pray for our leaders and respect them."

At these words, the officer calmed down. Boutros looked him in the eye and said, "God is love. And he loves you."

These words ended the interrogation. The officer scribbled down a phone number and slid it to Boutros.

"What is this?"

"My personal cell phone number. Let me know if you have any more trouble with the secret police."

Boutros thanked the man and stopped by the church to shower. After sharing his story, he headed home to his wife and child. The next day, he was back on the streets, proclaiming the gospel to all who would listen.

Believers such as Boutros risk everything to spread God's Word, even putting their lives in danger. Their stories of courage inspire us as we remember that Jesus said, "I have said these things to you, that in me you may have peace. In the world you will have tribulation. But take heart; I have overcome the world" (John 16:33).

Think of people you know who resist the gospel, as the secret police officer presumably did before he encountered Boutros. Pray that God will speak to their hearts so they will come to know and serve him. After all, God sees in them (as he does in each believer) the potential to exhibit what he sees in Boutros: a courageous faith that will not be deterred.

16

Courage to Seek the Truth

Amal
Israel

When Amal, a teenage Israeli Arab, returned home from school one day, she smelled something burning. Her mother had set her favorite book—her Bible—on fire. Again.

Nine times during a span of three years, her mother had burned her Bible to dissuade her from clinging to her Christian faith. This was among the milder reactions she would receive from her parents and siblings in a community in which Jesus followers often met intense resistance—including bodily harm—from their families.

Amal heard about Jesus when she was thirteen. She was struggling to find her way and was questioning the status quo. "I started to get real lost, and I reached a junction," she said later. *Which path will lead me to the truth—Islam or Christianity?*

Upon hearing of Amal's interest in Christianity, a high school teacher warned her to stay away from it because she could be killed.

"Okay, God," she prayed one night, "I want to ask you if you are the god of Islam. Just tell me that you are, and I will wear the hijab [head covering] and do all the prayers that you want. But if you are the God of Christians, even if this will lead me to be killed, I will still believe in you."

Then Amal dreamed about her search for life's answers. "In my dream, I woke up. There was so much light I couldn't look at it," she remembered. "The light, who I later realized was Jesus, told me to start walking. Every time I fell, he would grab my hand, pull me up, and continue walking. We reached an oasis. He asked me to grab a book out of the water. He said, 'The answer you are looking for is inside that book.' I read the verse where it says, 'I am the way and the truth and the life.'"

Fully awake now, she wondered, *Where did that verse come from? The Quran? The Bible? Somewhere else?* She searched diligently and discovered John 14:6 in the Bible, which stated those exact words. That was when she gave herself to the way and the truth and the life—Jesus Christ.

"Since then, I started to see how the Lord is working and how he is protecting me," she said. And she needed protection often. In addition to her mother burning her Bibles, her brother assaulted her when she was eighteen. She had returned home late one night after visiting a Christian in a hospital.

"Where were you?" he demanded.

"At the hospital."

"No, you are lying," he retorted. "You were at a service."

Surprised that her brother even knew the term for a gathering of Jesus followers, she repeated that she had been at the hospital. He grabbed her and smashed her head into a window, berating her with a torrent of words.

When her father arrived, she hoped he would intervene. Instead, he began to beat her too. She fled from the kitchen to the bathroom, but her brother dragged her into her bedroom and slapped her in the face. She fainted.

When she awoke a few minutes later, her family was wailing in anguish. Her father had just had a stroke. They blamed Amal for causing the stroke and forced her to stay in her room for two weeks. They took away her phone and identification and barely fed her. Her health deteriorated. When she fainted a second time, her family took her to the hospital.

Suspecting child abuse, medical workers called the police. Amal wanted to tell the police what really had happened but refused to do so.

"I wanted to be like a testimony and prove that I am God's daughter," she said.

After recovering, Amal moved out and began attending a Bible college. (She told her family she was studying social work.) On the day of her graduation, her father picked her up and promptly thrust a newspaper at her. He had seen a story and photograph about her earning a theology degree.

"Just ask God that your brother won't see the photo," he stated. He did not speak to her again for two months.

Despite her family's violent response to her faith, Amal had the courage to move back home. She led three of her sisters and younger brother (not the one who beat her) to the Lord. Slowly, healing has come to her family. Her parents now accept her faith, even though they don't personally embrace it.

Her older brother is married and no longer lives with the family. Still, he threatens her. "I am just waiting to do something to hurt you," he has warned.

Amal leads a group of people in their twenties who have converted from Islam to Christianity. The obstacles she has overcome are a testimony to how deeply rooted her faith is. Yes, on one hand her mother burned those Bibles and her family hurt her deeply. Yet she triumphed in her absolute resolve to replace her Bible every time it was burned and to keep sharing about Jesus.

It's painful enough to be opposed by someone we don't know. Imagine how difficult it was for Amal to be scorned and abused by her own family. No wonder she chose Jesus's unconditional love that doesn't ebb and flow based on circumstances. To those who are faithful and courageous, he says, "You are those who have stayed with me in my trials, and I assign to you, as my Father assigned to me, a kingdom, that you may eat and drink at my table in my kingdom" (Luke 22:28–30).

May God strengthen our resolve, and that of our persecuted family all over the world, to keep our eyes fixed on Jesus as we share our hope with those around us who desperately need the Savior who found us.

Martyrs in History

Wang Ming-Dao
1900–1991
China

If the apostles and those with them had been afraid of the threats of the Jews, then they would not have dared to preach and teach in Jesus' name. Where then would the church be today?

Wang Ming-Dao, referring to Acts 4:1–31

Wang Ming-Dao became a Christian at age fourteen while attending the London Missionary Society's primary school. As an outspoken Christian, he remained a thorn in the side of China's Communist Party from the 1950s through the 1970s. Unwilling to bend his Christian views to the party's liking, he spent a total of twenty-two years in prison between 1958 and 1980.

In the 1920s, Ming-Dao founded a church called the Christian Tabernacle. It was nondenominational and not dependent on foreign funds. He didn't want any such alliances to influence what the church believed or how its people worshipped.

When Japan occupied northern China from 1937 to 1945, it organized a Chinese federation that every church was required to join. Ming-Dao refused, putting his life on the line. The federation threatened him, but he stood nose to nose with the Japanese imperialists. He believed it was wrong to form an alliance that included nonbelievers.

When Chinese Communists attained power in 1949, they instituted a state-sponsored, state-controlled church that Ming-Dao would have nothing to do with. The Party continuously threatened him; he continuously refused to join. In 1955, the Party imprisoned him.

During interrogation, Ming-Dao was threatened with torture and execution. After months of such treatment, he was so mentally broken that he confessed to crimes he knew he hadn't committed and promised to support the party's state-controlled church upon his release. But after being granted his freedom and regaining his health, he again refused to join. He declared that he had committed none of the crimes to which he had confessed. He was locked up again, this time for twenty-two years. Once, he was offered release and refused it, insisting that the government owed him an apology.

He died in Shanghai in 1991, at age ninety-one. His refusal to compromise set the stage for what became China's house church movement. These small gatherings are considered illegal, and the police can interrupt them at any time.

In his writings, Ming-Dao highlighted Peter and John's refusal to be shaken by threats from Jewish leaders resulting from the rapid spread of the gospel. Having no crime for which to arrest the men, the Jews threatened them. "So they called them and charged them not to speak or teach at all in the name of Jesus" (Acts 4:18).

Peter and John not only continued to speak and teach, but they did so even more boldly. "Even if those with great authority do the threatening, courageous people do not recant," Ming-Dao wrote. "Because these two valiant men were not afraid of threats, they were entirely unaffected by them."

Ming-Dao learned that threats should not instill fear in believers. Instead, they should be catalysts for proclaiming our almighty God with greater courage and boldness.

Part III

JOY

Blessed are you when people hate you and when they exclude you
and revile you and spurn your name as evil, on account of the
Son of Man! Rejoice in that day, and leap for joy, for behold, your
reward is great in heaven; for so their fathers did to the prophets.

Luke 6:22–23

Joy is probably not the first emotional expression we associate with persecuted followers of Jesus. They may be tortured, abused, and imprisoned without trial. They may have friends and family members who have been killed for their faith. They may be forced to flee their homes, leaving behind everything they own and the communities they love. They may live in crowded tent cities with no hope of a better life. Yet joy is often what people notice most when they encounter these believers.

How is this possible? How can people who suffer so much be filled to overflowing with joy?

If we take seriously Jesus's teaching and example and consider the shared experiences of early Christian believers, the presence of joy in the face of persecution might not be so surprising. Jesus taught his followers to rejoice and leap for joy when they were hated, excluded, reviled, and considered to be evil for his sake. Why? Because they would be blessed and greatly rewarded for their suffering (Luke 6:22–23).

Jesus, no stranger to persecution and unspeakable suffering, modeled such joy in his life: "… who for the joy that was set before him endured the cross, despising the shame, and is seated at the right hand of the throne of God" (Hebrews 12:2). His example is a powerful antidote to discouragement and weariness of heart.

Our human nature tries to avoid suffering at all costs, but James 1:2–3 reminds persecuted Jesus followers that suffering has a purpose: "Count it all joy, my brothers, when you meet trials of various kinds, for you know that the testing of your faith produces steadfastness."

Certainly our brothers and sisters in the faith don't like to suffer, and we are pained by the fact that they do. But enduring persecution for the sake of Christ is far bigger than pain and suffering. It is about participating in God's ongoing redemptive work on earth and a glorious eternity with him.

Whether followers of Jesus experience joy in the midst of persecution has far more to do with where our focus is than on the circumstances we encounter. If our joy depends on happy life circumstances, we are in serious trouble when persecution comes. But the Bible is clear about focusing on a greater reality: "If then you have been raised with Christ, seek the things that are above, where Christ is, seated at the right hand of God. Set your minds on things that are above, not on things that are on earth" (Colossians 3:1–2).

This greater reality makes all the difference. It changes our perspective completely. It gives us joy that cannot be held back. That's why

Paul could write to his brothers and sisters in Christ, "You endured a hard struggle with sufferings … and you joyfully accepted the plundering of your property, since you knew that you yourselves had a better possession and an abiding one [in heaven]" (Hebrews 10:32, 34).

Such deep joy from God sets apart persecuted Jesus followers. Family members notice it. Neighbors notice it. Prison guards notice it. Even hardened ISIS fighters notice it. And that joy has an impact, sometimes leading even the persecutors to want to know the Jesus of those they persecute.

So read on and share in the joy of your brothers and sisters in Christ who count it a privilege to serve him.

17

Freedom behind Bars

Jon
Malaysia

A light breeze rustled through the palm trees, easing the ever-present heat that is as much a part of life in Malaysia as cold is in the Arctic. In a small suburb of Kuala Lumpur, a city of 1.6 million people and the sixth most visited city in the world, Jon concluded a Bible study with ten other ethnic Malay Christians.

As they said their good-byes outside, Jon felt good. The gathering had gone well. March clouds that often dumped buckets of rain were still far in the distance. He would have no trouble getting home before it rained. He looked forward to returning home, where he could turn on his fan and immerse himself more deeply into the Word of God.

Even when he saw the SUV speeding toward him, Jon didn't fret. He knew the drill. Since he had converted to Christianity six years earlier, he'd become accustomed to police harassment. Every three months, they made him report to them. They would urge him to recite Islamic prayers and re-embrace the Islamic faith and his ethnic heritage. And every three months, he'd politely refuse.

In Malaysia, the population includes a variety of ethnicities—Chinese, Vietnamese, Indians, and others. In addition, the Malaysian government strives to maintain a distinct, indigenous Malay culture that requires all Malay people to be Muslim. Two sets of laws exist for governing the people. Civil laws govern all citizens. Islamic laws concerning matters of religion, family, property, and inheritance apply only to Muslims.

It's illegal for Malay people to convert, and evangelization of Muslims is punishable by fine, imprisonment, or both. Although the number of converts to Jesus is increasing, there were no more than one thousand Malay Christians among Malaysia's population of twenty-eight million at the time of Jon's arrest in 2011.

Jon's boldness in following Jesus had made him a traitor in the eyes of most Malays. Yet thus far, police interactions with him had always had the air of going through the motions. He even knew the exact location where the police chief would hang his hat each day.

When the SUV screeched to a halt, Jon noticed a bit more bravado than usual. Still, he figured it was a routine three-month visit. Seconds later, three men grabbed him, blindfolded him, and threw him into the car. Then they pursued the others.

"No, no, no! Don't take them," Jon called out amid the bedlam. "Just take me. Do what you will with me, but leave them out of it."

The leader grabbed Jon's face, thumb on one side and four fingers on the other, squeezing it in a vise-like grip. "Our patience with you, rotten *kafir* [infidel], has run out. It is time for you to be rehabilitated. To return to what you never should have left: your faith in Allah!"

Islam, Jon knew, is more than a religion for indigenous Malays; it is their national identity. Muslims who try to leave Islam can be subjected to many hardships, including imprisonment in rehabilitation camps. So when the policeman used the word *rehabilitated*, Jon's mind turned to what might happen next.

Four hours later, he stumbled out of the SUV and into a walled compound in the northern Malaysia jungle near the border with Thailand. Barbed wire along the tops of fifteen-foot-high walls communicated that regardless of what happened inside, officials didn't want anyone leaving on their own.

Jon had heard of such places. They were called Islamic purification centers and were presented as "voluntary retreat centers" for Muslims who struggled with their faith. But Jon wasn't a voluntary guest. He was bound hand and foot and placed in a small room with three other men who he later learned were Christian converts.

Then his "purification" began.

Several times a day, long-bearded Islamic scholars interrogated him. They wanted him to chant with them. He refused.

"All I could hear," he said later, "was people praying for me."

They poured Islamic "holy water" over his head to "cleanse" him. When that didn't work, they used seven buckets of water. He refused to deny Jesus.

"You must embrace Islam again," a scholar declared.

"I will not," Jon replied. "Even if you chop off my head right now, it's okay. I have my God."

Angered by Jon's defiance, "rehab" workers beat him. When he was on the ground, they kicked his stomach and back.

"But I didn't feel any pain or humiliation," he recalled later. "I believe the Lord came, and I could hear angels and the prayers of my

Christian friends. When those men stepped on me and kicked me, that's when I felt the prayers; that's when I felt the presence of God."

After additional beating and kicking failed, the leaders switched to a new method to "cure" Jon of his conversion to Jesus. They forced him to sit naked on ice while men shouted verses from the Quran at him. "We are going to kill you if don't confess the Muslim prayer," one said.

Jon did not reply.

They beat him with a thick bamboo cane. "Say it!" another commanded.

Jon did not reply.

He was immersed, he said later, in a vision of Jesus himself being beaten. "I saw the blood of Jesus dripping, and then I heard the gentle voice of the Holy Spirit telling me not to deny Jesus no matter what."

Jon was so full of the Spirit that, at one point during the beatings, he actually began laughing—not to mock his torturers, but to express his joy for the honor he was feeling. "I was okay with being beaten," he recalled. "They beat Jesus too."

After three days of torture, the religious police released Jon into the custody of local authorities. Members of his church paid his bond, and he once again was free to feel the tropical breezes on his back and rejoice in his freedom in Christ.

Jon's joy rather than fear in the midst of his suffering might seem incredible to us. But such a response won't surprise us if we understand the power of faith and trust in Christ. "Do not fear what you are about to suffer," we read in Revelation 2:10. "Behold, the devil is about to throw some of you into prison, that you may be tested, and for ten days you will have tribulation. Be faithful unto death, and I will give you the crown of life."

By faith, Jon availed himself of the fullness of God's power, and his joy in the midst of suffering could not be contained. He didn't prevail because of deft argumentative skills. Or because he was physically stronger than most people. Or because he was craftier. He prevailed because he trusted God unwaveringly and prayed unceasingly—and because other Jesus followers prayed for him.

May we be faithful to pray for our persecuted family. Our prayers matter. Jesus followers like Jon depend on the prayers of their brothers and sisters in Christ to remain strong in their faith and experience the joy of God's Spirit.

18

Tested by Fire

Solomon
Nigeria

The assailants who attacked Solomon and his father, Inoma, were not militant Boko Haram insurgents who would sweep down from the north; nor were they Muslim Fulani herdsmen who had a penchant for attacking Christians. They were neighbors.

Muslim men whom the father and son knew and saw each day suddenly began shooting at them. Like fish in a barrel, Solomon and Inoma darted left and right seeking some sliver of cover. Bullets ricocheted everywhere. Other men wielding machetes joined in the attack. Even if the father and son had been armed, it still would not have been a fair fight.

A machete slammed down between Inoma's head and shoulder. The left side of his torso collapsed. He died instantly.

Seconds later, shocked, Solomon stopped and stared at his father's killer.

"We will not cut you if you turn back to Islam," stated the young man, bloody machete in hand.

"I will not," said Solomon.

"You are Christian. Where are you going? This is the end of the road. You have only one choice left: follow Islam."

"No," repeated Solomon.

Immediately, he felt liquid splash across his back. Gasoline fumes almost choked him.

"Now will you leave this Jesus for Allah?" the killer asked.

"I will not."

A blow to the back of his head knocked Solomon to the ground. Another attacker revved up a motorcycle and rode it onto Solomon's back, got off, and laid it—engine still running—on top of him. The attackers then ignited his gasoline-soaked shirt. Pinned to the ground by the weight of the motorcycle, Solomon could not escape the flames.

Sometime later, his mind foggy and body racked by pain, Solomon vaguely remembered being placed inside a four-wheel-drive vehicle for the agonizing, bumpy ride on snake-like roads to the hospital.

Solomon lived, but his back—even after numerous skin grafts—looks like scorched leather. Doctors have said his pain will never completely go away.

Considering all that he has suffered, Solomon's attitude might surprise us. He does not lament his disfigurement, the added difficulty it creates in his job as a carpenter, or that his wife-to-be fled after the attack. "She doesn't believe I have a future," he said. With hopeful trust in God, he continued, "I would like prayer that I will again gain my strength and that God will bring into my life another lady. I understand that she left because, perhaps, she was not God's will for me."

Despite what he has endured, Solomon is not bitter or discouraged. "I won't turn back," he said with confidence. "The salvation that I have in Christ was not free but paid with a price. Christ himself suffered to save me, so I feel I am prepared to suffer in persecution for the salvation I have in Christ."

If Solomon were to see his attackers again, which is a real possibility in the African bush where he now lives, he would say the same thing Jesus said while on the cross: "Father, forgive them." He wants his attackers to know that the God they despise died for their sins too.

Through persecution and suffering, Solomon has gained a faith that is more precious than gold. "Based on what happened to me," he said, "it is a miracle that I survived. I know that my life is in God's hands, so what happened to me has strengthened my relationship with him."

This is the kind of faith in the face of persecution that Peter, Jesus's disciple, described in 1 Peter 1:6–7: "In this you rejoice, though now for a little while, if necessary, you have been grieved by various trials, so that the tested genuineness of your faith—more precious than gold that perishes though it is tested by fire—may be found to result in praise and glory and honor at the revelation of Jesus Christ."

Rejoice in such testing? Yes!

Jesus considered it joy to remain faithful to the cross and die for the sins of all humanity. Around the world, the fires of hatred lick at our persecuted brothers and sisters like Solomon. Yet they stand firm in their faith—no matter what the price—and experience a deep trust and joy in knowing God in a way that only those who remain faithful can.

May we stand with them, praying for them and rejoicing in a genuine faith that brings praise, honor, and glory to Jesus.

19

Daring to Speak the Truth

Musa
North Africa

The question hung in the air like words frozen in fear.

It was a cold February day. On a construction site, a coworker and beloved friend of Musa had become suspicious of Musa's unwillingness to kneel in prayer at the prescribed hours like everyone else.

"Why don't you take a break when it's time for prayer like the rest of us? It's your right, and you can have some rest."

To many people in the West, this question might seem insignificant. But this was North Africa, where Islam rules with a heavy hand. Not participating in religious practices can trigger scorn. Defying the faith can trigger terrible suffering.

Musa realized, *This is it.* This was the moment he had to decide if he was for Christ or against him. A phony or the real deal. All in or all out.

After a long pause, he looked his friend in the eye. "Prayer," he began, "is an intimate conversation with God, and it should be done all the time, in my heart, rather than at specific times using the same phrases and postures."

His friend's eyes narrowed. "You can't be serious, can you?" he questioned, then laughed uneasily. "You are joking with me, aren't you, my friend?"

Musa shook his head. He didn't want to hurt his friend, but he would not lie. "I am quite serious. I am a follower of Christ."

His friend glanced around as if not wanting anyone else to hear. Denial turned to surprise, then to anger. "You have lost your mind, Musa!" he exclaimed. "You have become a *kafir*!"

"I am who God wants me to be," Musa answered confidently. "He wants the same for you. He created you and longs to have a personal relationship with—"

"Shut up, Musa! I am proud to be a Muslim. You don't deserve my friendship."

"But I hope to keep our friendship," said Musa.

"You are dead to me. I hope you repent and come back to the true way of Allah and his prophet, Muhammad." Then he turned and left.

A few days later, the construction site supervisor called Musa into the office and asked, "Is this true? Are you now a Christian?"

"I am," said Musa, realizing that his friend had betrayed him.

"Then you are fired for proselytizing—"

"But I have not tried to convert anyone."

"Get out," the supervisor ordered. "No pension. No severance. No final month's wages. Begone, you traitor."

As he headed home, Musa reflected on how much easier—though not better—his life would be had he not chosen to follow Christ.

When he was in his early twenties, Musa had questioned the Muslim faith he'd been raised with. He had become uneasy with Islam's view of justice that permitted people to be hurt and even murdered in the name of Allah. Nearly a decade passed, however, before his doubt led him to faith in Christ.

At the age of thirty-five, married with three children, Musa did something nobody in his family had ever done: accepted Christ as his Lord and Savior. From that moment on, he knew he had become a wanted man. Even if he never doubted his decision to follow Christ, he would always be looking over his shoulder.

He even feared telling his wife, Farrah, about his faith because she might leave and take their children. So he prayed that she, too, would see the wonder of Jesus and embrace him. He began bringing home Christian literature from a library almost one hundred miles away and watching Christian television broadcasts.

When he finally told Farrah about his faith in Jesus, she recoiled in fear. "What if our relatives find out?" she exclaimed. "What then?"

Soon, however, after seeing a change for the better in her husband, she invited Jesus into her life. For two years, the couple told no one about their new faith. Then Musa was fired from his construction job, and now he worried about how he could provide for his family.

Not long after he returned home, the phone rang. A man offered Musa another construction job, which seemed like a miracle. "Could you meet with me this afternoon?"

"I thought it was the answer to my prayers," Musa said later. He became uneasy, however, when he realized that the meeting location was an abandoned building, not a construction site.

He had come to an ambush, not a job offer. Two men tried to force him to the back of the property, but Musa refused to leave the main road. The men began peppering him with questions about turning his back on Allah. Then they replaced their words with fists—to the stomach, face, and ribs. He began to wonder if he would leave the place alive.

Suddenly, a car approached and screeched to a halt. The attackers stopped their beating. Someone in the car opened a door and yelled, "Get in! We will help you."

Amazingly, news of Musa's faith and firing already had spread throughout the small Christian community that rallied to help him.

"He is a *kafir!*" yelled his tormentors as the car sped away. "He is a Christian and an evangelist!"

Days later, the same two assailants showed up in his neighborhood and spread the news that Musa had rejected Allah. Neighbors then turned against him too.

"If you do not go to the mosque and publicly recant your Jesus," one declared, "we will throw you out of your home. You are not welcome here if you are not of Allah."

Again, Christians came to help. "Come with us," someone said. "We have a safe place for you and your family to live." So the family loaded their possessions into the back of a pickup truck and left their home behind.

"I felt blessed when this happened to me," Musa said. At the truth-or-lie crossroads, he had dared to choose Jesus. He had counted the cost and dared to put everything at risk when he answered, "Yes, I am a follower of Christ."

That choice changes us and opens us up to experience the joy of the Lord. It is why the apostle Paul could experience joy and freedom even as his persecution intensified. "From now on let no one cause me trouble," he wrote, "for I bear on my body the marks of Jesus" (Galatians 6:17).

Daily, our persecuted brothers and sisters in the faith bear the marks of the Lord Jesus. They consider it a joy to remain true to him, regardless of the cost. Like Musa, they stand strong in their convictions and true to God's Word. "When the persecution came," Musa said, "my faith was tested and I learned much more to trust the Lord."

Such is the power of joy. May the example of our family in Jesus encourage us also to be willing to give up everything for what is truly valuable. May we be bold in choosing whom we will trust and serve.

20

Choosing Joy over Bitterness

Gulnaz
Pakistan

Gulnaz is a young married Christian woman who worked at a phone center. One day a Muslim man came in to make a call and refused to leave. He then made sexual advances toward her. When she slapped him, he vowed that he would make her pay for her "disrespect."

Unfortunately, young Christian women in Pakistan often drink from a very bitter cup of suffering. Some men take pleasure in exerting power over these women for their own shameful satisfaction. They treat them as nothing more than possessions to be used and discarded. Gulnaz suffered such abuse. Her would-be attacker returned and poured acid on her, badly burning her face, chest, and arms. But her story of faith and joy will not go untold. Christian medical personnel helped to provide treatment for her injuries, including surgery that enabled greater use of her severely damaged arm.

As she slowly healed from her wounds, Gulnaz experienced renewal and growth in her spiritual life as well. Instead of dwelling on her attack and the terrible scarring that resulted, Gulnaz and her husband kept their eyes firmly fixed on God. They refused to allow their circumstances to weigh them down in bitterness. Out of her tragedy emerged a triumph of God-breathed love and joy over hate.

Gulnaz and her husband live in a rundown neighborhood with open sewage in the streets and garbage piled everywhere. Looking at the needs around her, Gulnaz began witnessing to young girls. She even started a small Bible study for them.

When Christians gave Gulnaz and her husband a home in a much nicer area, the couple instead gave the keys to a Pakistani evangelist who was forced to live on the run after radical Muslims targeted his ministry. The home would have been very comfortable for the couple to live in, or they could have sold it for money they needed. But they figured the evangelist needed the home more than they did.

The generosity and joy they express in the wake of the pain they endure are an inspiration to anyone who faces even the least bit of persecution.

In situations such as Gulnaz's, it is easy to allow the circumstances or the people who try to control us to define us. But if we are followers of Jesus, our approval comes from him alone. Romans 10:11 reminds us, "Whoever believes on Him [Jesus] will not be put to shame" (NKJV). Jesus loves us unconditionally, and by focusing on him rather than our circumstances, we can walk through persecution with joy and hope.

However, not one of us can stand firm in our own strength. Paul wrote, "Finally, be strong in the Lord and in the strength of his might. Put on the whole armor of God, that you may be able to stand against the schemes of the devil. For we do not wrestle against flesh and blood, but against the rulers, against the authorities, against the cosmic powers over this present darkness, against the spiritual forces of evil in the heavenly places" (Ephesians 6:10–12).

Our family members in the global body of Christ need our faithful prayers for God's protection over them. Let us pray that they not only stand firm in their faith but also stand tall in the joy of Jesus's love for them. Let us continue to pray not only for their physical protection but also for their spiritual protection in the battles they fight. May the joy of their relationship with Jesus have an impact even on those who persecute and demean them.

21

An Unexplainable Escape

Farid
Afghanistan

It was 5:00 a.m. Inside the apartment, a handful of bearded men, heads wrapped in white or beige turbans, sat in a circle as if gathered around a campfire. What drew them together? Not the warmth of a fire, but the light of God's Word. Positioned on the floor in the middle of their circle, like the hub of a wheel, were hand-sketched illustrations of Bible stories. Nearby, a turquoise pitcher of water and matching basin had been prepared for foot washing. This was a Bible study.

In a tone just above a whisper, Farid, the group leader, prayed, "We thank you, God, for your willingness to meet with us this morning. We thank you for your presence here among us."

Outside the apartment, Afghanistan's harsh and rugged landscape awakened with first light. The city's buildings blended in with the steep, rising mountains beyond, all colored in sandy shades of brown. It was difficult to tell where humanity ended and nature began.

Farid had just introduced the book of Acts when someone pounded on the door. Before anyone could react, dark-clothed intruders burst in brandishing rifles and knives. Farid was slammed to the floor. His hands were tied behind his back, and a knife was placed just inches from his neck. None of the six men resisted.

Amid the panic and confusion came clarity in prayer. "God," Farid prayed, "if this is the time for me to die, I forgive these people who want to kill me."

Farid believed it was an honor to die for God's glory. If he died, he didn't want the intruders' blood on his hands. "I wanted God to forgive them, and I wanted them to come to Christ as a result of my death," he said later.

He closed his eyes, waiting for the prick of intense pain and the end. When nothing happened, he sensed God wanting him to stand up and leave the room. So he stood. His hands were no longer tied. The straps simply fell to the floor. He walked toward the door, which was guarded by two armed men.

"Sit down, dog," one commanded. "You're not leaving—alive."

The other pointed his AK-47 rifle at Farid and squeezed the trigger.

Click. Nothing. The rifle had jammed.

Click. Again.

The rifle's failure to fire diverted both guards' attention, and Farid fled. As he raced down the stairs three or four steps at a time, he heard gunfire. He saw bullets chip the wall beyond him, but he escaped unharmed.

The story of his escape is even more amazing in light of the fact that none of his five companions were injured. Only the leader of the terrorist group was hurt when he was shot accidentally. In addition, the police made a chilling discovery during their investigation: inside a bag they found an al-Qaida flag, two swords, and a video camera.

According to police, the terrorists had planned to videotape the beheading of all six men and show it on the Al Jazeera television network. Evidently, the attackers knew Farid was winning Afghan Muslims to Christ. The videotape would warn missionaries, evangelists, and former Muslims that they would be killed if they didn't stop their evangelism and discipleship. Although the Constitution of Afghanistan reads, "Followers of other religions are free to exercise their faith and perform their religious rites within the limits of the provisions of the law," violence trumps the law.

"This is a Muslim country, and men fighting for Islam have issued these threats for twenty-five years," Farid explained. As Jesus followers in Afghanistan know all too well, "they don't like non-Muslim people coming in to preach. In the Quran, it is written that if somebody rejects Islam, you must kill them."

What terrorists wanted to accomplish that morning did not happen. Heads did not roll. Blood was not spilled. The only casualty was one of their own, even though none of the six Christians resisted with force.

Instead, followers of Jesus experienced yet another reason to rejoice in the awesome power of their sovereign God. No wonder the apostle Paul rejoiced in his suffering and wrote of his desire to "know him [Jesus] and the power of his resurrection, and may share his sufferings, becoming like him in his death" (Philippians 3:10).

The power of the resurrection gives all who follow Jesus reason for great joy. That power is at work in the lives of every Jesus follower who risks persecution and suffering in order to walk faithfully with him. What a gift to know and believe that our God is without limits and that he is in control of everything that happens to us. Let us join with our persecuted brothers and sisters in Christ and rejoice in the power and faithfulness of our sovereign God. May our joy in Christ ever increase as we grow in trust and faith in him.

22

The Former Witch Doctor

Abdul Masih

Nigeria

Abdul Masih was a Fulani Muslim witch doctor. In the 1980s, when he was young, he traveled from village to village prescribing herbal remedies and chanting incantations over sick or injured people. An innate curiosity about people drew him into this practice. *What made them sick?* he wondered. *What might make them well?*

After five years as a witch doctor, that same curiosity drew him to ask questions about Christians. *What God do they worship? What do they believe? How are they different from those of us who are Muslim?*

He began his quest by reading what the Quran said about "Isa," as Jesus is referred to in that book. He was surprised to discover that the Quran makes fewer references to Muhammad, the writer and author of the Quran, than it does to Jesus. That worried him.

So he began a secret search for Christians so he could learn more. It was not easy because in the Katsina State where he lived, Christians are as rare as snowflakes. But he found a few and asked to speak to their pastor.

Understandably, they were leery—even afraid. Nigerian Muslims often attack Jesus followers. At first these believers wondered if Abdul intended to expose and persecute them. In time, they were convinced he was genuinely interested in their faith, so they escorted him to their pastor's house.

The pastor, too, was afraid. A Muslim witch doctor meeting with a Christian pastor? He didn't like the setup. In fact, after Abdul showed up, the pastor refused to meet with him. But Abdul would not be deterred. He was so eager to meet the pastor that he went to his home at 4:00 a.m.

Surprised but also impressed, the pastor relaxed. *This witch doctor is sincere in his quest for the truth*, he realized. So the two men began meeting regularly. Six weeks into their meetings, Abdul professed faith in Jesus.

News of Abdul's conversion spread quickly. Rumors that Abdul had accepted 250,000 naira (about $1,500) to become a Jesus follower and had given the "infidels" his Quran to be burned triggered intense anger among local Muslims. To protect Abdul, church leaders arranged for him to leave town.

When the rumors reached Abdul's home village and family, his brother decided to kill Abdul to save the family's honor. He discovered the new village where Abdul lived and walked to it. Upon seeing his brother, Abdul thought something had happened to their parents and his brother was bringing the news.

"That's not why I have come," stated his brother. "I just want to confirm if what I have heard is true. If it is, I will execute you and go back home."

"You want to kill your own brother?" asked Abdul.

His brother nodded.

"Yes, I am a Christian," Abdul confirmed.

"Why would you accept the little sum of 250,000 naira to convert your faith and give your Quran to the infidels to torch?"

"That is a lie," Abdul said. "I have done no such thing."

Abdul's brother did not kill him that day. In fact, he eventually accepted Jesus as his Lord and Savior. And furthermore, all of his brother's children accepted Jesus, including one who now attends Bible school and plans to become a pastor.

Life for this family of Jesus followers in northern Nigeria is not easy. Islamic Shariah law rules the land, and publicly sharing their faith can be dangerous. Yet they continue to share privately with anyone who will listen.

Abdul has discovered that he has a special rapport with Muslim clerics, who always listen to his message. "The cleric will understand you, and you will understand him," said Abdul, "because deep in his heart he knows the truth." The same truth, the same power, that turned a witch doctor into an evangelist for Christ can also change the heart of a Muslim cleric.

Other Muslims remain hostile to Abdul, however. Islamic extremists have tried to kill him at least three times. "There is no fear in my heart," he said. In fact, there is contentment, hope, and even joy in the opportunity persecution creates to bring glory to Christ. "I know that if I'm dead I'm going to be with the Lord. So I'm not afraid to die. My greatest desire now is to be an instrument to preach the gospel of the Lord Jesus so that the Muslims can hear it."

And a few do hear it. When someone takes the step of faith in Jesus, Abdul rejoices but does not sugarcoat what the new believer will face in the days ahead. "You have come to suffer," he says, and often shares 2 Timothy 3:12 with them: "Indeed, all who desire to live a godly life in Christ Jesus will be persecuted."

The promise of persecution is difficult, but it does not diminish the joy of following Jesus. For those who place their faith in Christ, true hope lies far beyond the security, ease, and comfort of this world. It lies far beyond the way people treat us in this life.

For the follower of Jesus, true hope rests in the strength of the one who sustains us in this world and provides a home for us in heaven. True joy comes when our affections are set so firmly in eternity that we consider any affliction that comes because of our commitment to Christ to be a privilege.

By God's grace, may we begin to see persecution as an opportunity to serve and honor our Savior. May we accept persecution with a heart of joy and hope. May the needs and struggles of our brothers and sisters in Christ who face the hardships of persecution today always be on our hearts and in our prayers.

23

No Longer on the Sidelines

Akhom and Hassani

Egypt

This night would not be like other nights. Something big was happening. The old men who usually gathered at the corner cafés each night to smoke shisha and play board games were gone. In their place, hundreds of Egyptian Christians began walking peacefully through the streets of the Coptic neighborhood of Mokattam.

Together they walked to mark the end of forty days of mourning following sectarian clashes that had killed twenty-seven people, most of them Jesus followers. Not knowing what the cost might be, they proudly identified themselves with Jesus in a Muslim world. By standing together, they were making a powerful statement to anyone in the world who was paying attention.

Since the January-February revolution that led to more than eight hundred people being killed and more than six thousand injured, Egypt had been awash in social, political, and cultural turmoil. Everywhere, it seemed, people were standing up for what they believed—or standing up to silence the beliefs of others.

The Christian community in Egypt has come under repeated attack since the 2011 revolution—by both the Egyptian military and Muslim extremists. This level of persecution has shocked the Christian community in Egypt. Some of the attacks even took place in Mokattam. In one of those attacks on March 8, 2011, two cousins were severely injured.

Twenty-one-year-old Akhom considered himself to be a Christian but knew that his spiritual life was more going through the motions than a serious commitment. One night he found himself caught in a situation that quickly turned from peace to turmoil. Attackers started throwing rocks, bricks, and broken glass from a six-story apartment building. Clashes broke out. Suddenly, a man fired three shots into Akhom's face and one into his stomach. His cousin Hassani was also injured that night when an attacker cut his face with a machete.

Both men survived, which some consider a miracle. As they healed in a hospital, made possible by Christians who paid their medical expenses and supported them in prayer, they recognized a greater miracle. The brutal attack they suffered and the horrible wounds they still endured led them to fully commit their lives to Jesus.

Akhom's shattered jaw had to be stabilized and anchored with screws. His stomach is scarred from the bullet and the incisions to retrieve it. But the destruction of his body led to a renewal of his spirit.

"The attack helped me to get closer to God," he said. "I was away from the Lord. I was doing bad things, living a life of sin. While I was healing, I was always asking the Lord to change me, to make more perfection in my heart."

The pain he suffered wasn't without meaning; it was pain infused with the joy of a more intimate relationship with Jesus.

"Persecution is part of our faith," Akhom said. Referring to the life of Jesus, he explained, "He was persecuted, and he told us in the world we would suffer. But he made sure we knew he overcame the world, so we are following the same model. We have to rejoice in what the Bible tells us. If persecution happens in our life, then it is a privilege to us. It means we are going the right way. We couldn't see it before, but now I see our trials the Lord allowed us to have. This is strengthening our faith."

Hassani experienced a similar transformation. His injuries required months of painful reconstructive surgery on his face, but even more significant was the "reconstructive surgery" on his heart.

"Before the attack, I did not have any time to be with the Lord to pray," he recalled. "God was not there in my life. I did not know him as a Good Shepherd. But a new vision came after the attack. My heart was opened to realize the grace of the Lord. I now see him as a Good Shepherd because it is a miracle I am alive!"

With joy, he thanks God for the prayers and medical assistance other Christians provided during his time of need.

"It is exactly as the Bible says," Hassani continued. "I can never forget the blessing God sent to me. Because of him, I'm alive. He showed me mercy."

Now, Hassani said, he must do the same with his attackers. He seeks to follow the example of Jesus: "For to this you have been called, because Christ also suffered for you, leaving you an example, so that you might follow in his steps. He committed no sin, neither was deceit found in his mouth. When he was reviled, he did not revile in return; when he suffered, he did not threaten, but continued entrusting himself to him who judges justly" (1 Peter 2:21–23).

No longer playing it "safe," no longer experiencing the emptiness of a halfhearted commitment to Jesus, Hassani and Akhom choose to trust in Jesus and stand for him in a country where his message is not welcome. They walk in the confidence of 2 Timothy 1:7: "For God gave us a spirit not of fear but of power and love and self-control."

Armed with the power of God's love and filled with the joy of knowing Jesus, Hassani spoke for both of them when he said, "We are praying for those persecutors who are killing us, that they may know the truth. I feel sorry for them and for those who are far from the Lord. *They* are really suffering."

Martyrs in History

Mehdi Dibaj
1935–1994
Iran

I have always envied those Christians who were martyred for Christ Jesus our Lord. What a privilege to live for our Lord and to die for Him as well. I am filled to overflowing with joy; I am not only satisfied to be in prison ... but am ready to give my life for the sake of Jesus Christ.
Mehdi Dibaj

After his arrest in 1984, Rev. Mehdi Dibaj spent nine years in prison. Even there, he considered it a privilege to live for his Lord and was filled with joy at the prospect of dying for him as well. Finally, on December 3, 1993, Dibaj addressed the court in the city of Sari to defend himself for embracing Christianity. "I am ready to give my life for the sake of Jesus," he said. In his defense, he addressed four accusations that the court had made against him:

- "They say, 'You were a Muslim and you have become a Christian.' This is not so. For many years I had no religion. After searching and studying, I accepted God's call and believed in the Lord Jesus Christ in order to receive eternal life. People choose their religion, but a Christian is chosen by Christ, who says, 'You have not chosen me, but I have chosen you.'"

- "People say, 'You were a Muslim from your birth.' God says, 'You were a Christian from the beginning.' He states that He chose us thousands of years ago, even before the creation of the universe, so that through the sacrifice of Jesus Christ we may be His."

- "They tell me, 'Return.' But to whom can I return from the arms of God? Is it right to accept what people are saying instead of obeying the Word of God? It is now forty-five years that I am walking with the God of miracles, and His kindness upon me is like a shadow and I owe Him much for His fatherly love and concern."

- "They object to my evangelizing. But if one finds a blind person who is about to fall into a well and keeps silent, then one has sinned. It is our religious duty, as long as the door of God's mercy is open, to convince evildoers to turn from their sinful ways and find refuge in Him."

About three weeks after Dibaj made his defense, the court declared him guilty of apostasy for abandoning Islam and embracing Christianity. They ordered his death. Dibaj had been a disciple of Jesus for forty-five years when the court condemned him to die.

Outraged by Dibaj's death sentence, an Armenian minister, Bishop Haik Hovsepian, told the media about what he viewed as an unfathomable injustice. He thought that if enough public pressure were placed on Islamic authorities, they might overturn Dibaj's sentence.

He knew the effort created great risk. "If we go to jail or die for our faith," he said, "we want the whole Christian world to know what is happening to their Christian brothers and sisters."

On January 16, 1994, Hovsepian's efforts bore fruit. Dibaj was released. But the joyous celebration was short lived. Only three days later, Hovsepian went missing. Weeks passed before authorities reported that he had been killed. Then, five months later, Dibaj was abducted and killed on his way to his daughter's birthday gathering. Muslim extremists also killed Rev. Tateos Michaelian, Hovsepian's replacement as chairman of the Council of Protestant Ministers.

But what the Islamic authorities believed would silence and intimidate the global church, especially Muslim converts to Christianity, ended up doing the opposite. These martyrdoms drew the attention of more Iranians to the gospel and led to an increasing number of conversions from Islam to Christianity. Today more Muslims are coming to Christ than ever before in the history of the church. Yes, there is joy in giving up everything for Jesus.

Part IV

PERSEVERANCE

*And you will be hated by all for my name's sake. But
the one who endures to the end will be saved.*

Mark 13:13

From beginning to end, the Bible is full of promises for those who
faithfully seek to know and serve the living God. We often look to
such promises for encouragement when we encounter difficulties in
life, particularly when we face challenges in our walk with God. But
take a look at the promise of 2 Timothy 3:12: "Indeed, all who desire
to live a godly life in Christ Jesus will be persecuted." And Mark
13:13: "And you will be hated by all for my name's sake. But the one
who endures to the end will be saved."

What promises! The certainty of persecution isn't the kind of
encouragement most of us hope to find in God's Word. But if persecution is a reality for all who live a Christ-centered life, then we
certainly need encouragement. We need to learn how to endure to
the end. To persevere for the cause of Jesus Christ means to stand
firm and resist whatever opposition rises against us. The picture that
comes to mind is that of a person who leans into and stands against

a strong wind or plants his feet and pushes back against a powerful river current.

Persecuted followers of Jesus learn quickly that it's impossible to persevere in their own strength. Jesus knew it would be that way. During the last Passover meal he shared with his disciples, he talked about how necessary it would be for them to remain in a life-giving relationship with him. He said bluntly, "As the branch cannot bear fruit by itself, unless it abides in the vine, neither can you, unless you abide in me. I am the vine; you are the branches … apart from me you can do nothing" (John 15:4–5).

If we want to be followers of Jesus who stand firm in service to him, we, too, must abide in him. We must be rooted in the character and Word of God. We must cling to that relationship, growing closer to him, experiencing more of who he is, and discovering what it means to walk with him in faith. As our intimacy with God grows, his strength empowers us to obey and endure faithfully regardless of the cost.

David had a heart that earnestly pursued a relationship with God. In Psalm 40:1–2, he wrote about the strength that relationship provided in the face of pain and adversity: "I waited patiently for the LORD; he inclined to me and heard my cry. He … set my feet upon a rock, making my steps secure."

Joseph, an early Bible patriarch, spent many years enslaved and imprisoned. Despite the suffering he endured at the hands of people who mistreated him, lied about him, and forgot about him, God was with him (Genesis 39:2). Rather than removing Joseph from his suffering, God empowered him to stand firm, to learn to trust and obey him in everything. Later, Joseph played an important role as God unfolded his plans and purposes in establishing the ancient nation of Israel.

Every day in communities in Iraq and other countries where Islamic extremists exert control, Jesus followers stand firm in their commitment to trust God and obediently fulfill his purpose for their lives. They pay a high personal price for persevering in their faith. They endure fierce hostility, brutal cruelty, and unthinkable atrocities, yet they remain true to God. As you read their stories, notice how the strength of their relationship with their Lord and Savior empowers them to "run with endurance the race" that is set before them (Hebrews 12:1).

24

Prayers to Escape and Prayers to Endure

Abdi
Somalia

When his captors began beating Abdi, they removed his blindfold. They wanted him to see why the underground cell where he was being held smelled so bad. They wanted to ratchet up his fear. It worked.

Whack! Abdi could never forget the macabre sight of the three dead bodies that were piled, contorted, in the corner. He shuddered in terror, waiting for the next blow.

Whack! Another shot to his back with the wooden baton.

"God, save me," he whispered. "Save my life."

Whack! Everything went dark.

The previous night, Abdi had gone to sleep in his one-room house, his wife and three children sleeping near him. He had looked forward to another day to live for God and be faithful to whatever God had in store for him. However, Abdi slept in Somalia, where many people see the God of the Bible as bad news, not good news.

Abdi awoke suddenly to the sound of boots on the concrete floor. As if straight from a nightmare, four al-Shabab soldiers dressed in black were pointing a Russian-made machine gun and AK-47 assault rifles at him.

"Get up, apostate!" commanded one. The others rummaged through the family's possessions, searching for something. His wife cowered in a corner, and their children cried.

A soldier shoved a gun barrel closer to his head. "What profession are you, scum?" the intruder asked. "Where do you work?"

Suddenly, one soldier searched his bag and pulled pages of a Bible from it, a cross displayed prominently on each one. Another soldier grabbed Abdi by the neck and pushed him outside. The other two shoved him to the ground, tied his hands behind his back, and blindfolded him. He knew that simply possessing pages from a Bible could lead to imprisonment or death.

They forced Abdi into a truck and sped away.

Abdi's wife immediately contacted their Christian friends. "Please pray hard," she said. "Abdi has been taken. Pray that he can escape."

Hours later, Abdi's torture began.

"Where did you get this?" a captor asked, ripping the Bible pages. "Do you know others like you? Who are they?"

Whack! Another shot to his back with the wooden baton. *Whack!*

Then came his prayer and the temporary relief of unconsciousness.

During each day that followed, Abdi endured what seemed like endless pain.

The stench in his cell grew worse because he had no toilet. After ten days, soldiers removed the well-decayed corpses to make room for two new prisoners. Their arrival brought Abdi a splinter of light in the darkness.

One day the guards permitted all three men to be outside for a few hours. Thankful to breathe fresh air, Abdi studied the mud-walled compound and noticed what his cellmates also observed: a wall they might be able to climb.

That night in their cell, they plotted a "what do we have to lose?" escape. They knew they would need a special opportunity to make it happen. And they got it.

Several nights later, the guards accidentally left the cell door unlocked. The trio waited a few minutes and then bolted out of their cell and headed for the wall.

At the wall, soldiers started shooting. One prisoner went down. Abdi and the other man slipped over the top and raced into the night, threading their way through alleyways to lose the pursuing soldiers.

At home, the phone rang. Abdi's wife nearly fainted when she heard the voice she thought she'd never hear again.

"It cannot be possible!" she exclaimed. "Where are you? Are you really alive?" She cried and screamed, then raced to meet him and take him to the hospital.

Abdi had several broken bones. His arm was placed in a cast. As he recovered, Abdi continued to trust in Jesus. Nearly a year later, he still felt the pain of incarceration and escape—and the peace of Christ within.

"I was happy to go through all this because now I am stronger spiritually," he said. "People prayed for me to escape. Their prayers are what saved my life."

Abdi became a leader in the Somali Christian community and was known for his strong, enduring faith. He also led several Muslims to Christ. His perseverance in serving Christ did not go unnoticed. Although he was careful about how he traveled and what he exposed his family to, Abdi paid the ultimate price for his outspoken witness in December 2013. As he drove to work, members of al-Shabab surrounded his car and sprayed it with bullets.

Police pulled his lifeless body from the driver seat. Abdi had escaped before, but this time he endured to the end: "And you will be hated by all for my name's sake. But the one who endures to the end will be saved" (Mark 13:13).

May we pray unceasingly for our persecuted family members who endure so much because of their faith in Jesus. Our hope rests in our all-powerful God, who provides everything we need to stand for him and who can do what we cannot. It is our privilege to stand with our brothers and sisters in Christ and pray—for them both to escape and to endure as God wills.

25

The Boy Who Would Not Back Down

Hussein B.

Turkey

At his school in Turkey, nine-year-old Hussein fumbled excitedly with the clasp on his necklace. After fastening it around his neck, he straightened the cross pendant. He was proud to let his teachers and fellow students know of his new Christian faith.

The feeling would not be mutual.

In his innocence, Hussein didn't know that 96 percent of Turks are Muslim. Although many do not practice their faith, most believe that all Turks should be Muslim. He didn't know that practicing another religious faith is culturally unacceptable. He didn't know that despite government claims of religious tolerance, Jesus followers are not welcome in many parts of his country.

Hussein knew none of that the morning he first put on the cross. He knew only that his father, a former Islamic scholar, loved Jesus and so did he. His faith was as real to him as the cross he'd just placed around his neck.

"I felt so alive hearing the hymns and singing in the church," he said, describing his first time in a church. "I felt I had to learn more about this. I was so joyful, and I thought this might be my last time in church. So I opened the hymnal and thought about tearing the pages out and keeping them. I did not take them, but I wanted to so badly."

A year later, he decided to wear the cross, in part because he thought it could be a good way to talk with other students about his faith. "It's not the physical cross; it's the meaning of the cross," the precocious boy shared later. "It is a beautiful thing. I wanted people to ask me about it so I could tell them about Christ."

He did not anticipate the danger that wearing the cross would incite. Some students spit on the cross. Other students swore at him. "Stinkin' *kafir*," they called out. They threatened him because he embraced the dreaded "religion of the West."

One of his sisters told their parents about the cross. "Hussein is telling everyone that we are Christians!"

Hakeem, his father, bristled. "Don't *ever* tell people that you have become a Christian," he warned. "You don't want to get us into trouble. You must not wear that to school again!"

Later, Hakeem and his wife decided they had been wrong to force their son to suppress his faith. They realized that both of them had suppressed *their* faith and that Hussein's boldness, naive and idealistic as it was, should be celebrated, not condemned.

"We were trying to prevent conflicts with others, but we came to the realization that we were the ones with a problem," Hakeem said. "We decided to be like Hussein, more open about our Christianity."

Although his parents now supported Hussein's desire to tell others about his faith, his classmates continued to taunt him. He threatened to go to the principal if the abuse didn't stop. One boy grabbed him by the arm, squeezed his hand hard, and threatened, "I'm going to *shoot you* if you tell about this."

After Hussein described this incident, Hakeem went to the other boy's father. "I thought the father would be concerned about his son's actions," Hakeem said. "But instead, he called me a *kafir*, threatened me, and said he would shoot me himself if I pursued action against his son."

So the attacks continued. A gang of boys jumped on Hussein, threw rocks at him, and beat him with sticks. He screamed in pain as a boy dragged him along the ground by his shirt. The attack stopped only when Hakeem arrived to pick up his son.

The opposition to Hussein's faith grew even stronger. When Hakeem asked his son if he was still getting beaten up, the boy nodded.

"By whom?" his father asked.

"By my religion teacher," Hussein replied.

His religion teacher was an imam, an Islamic leader, who led worship in the neighborhood mosque. Every student in his class was required to write and recite the *shahada*: "There is no god but Allah, and Muhammad is his prophet."

Hussein refused to do it. In response, the teacher repeatedly struck him with a wooden rod. The boy endured persistent beatings for continuing not to recite the *shahada*.

"It isn't in my heart," Hussein said. "It's just meaningless words to me."

After three weeks of such beatings, Hussein had a seizure. Then another. And another. When Hakeem went to the school to confront the teacher, he found the man standing over his student, holding the rod.

The teacher stared at Hakeem. "Are you aware," he stated icily, "that your son is wearing a cross to school? Are you Christians?"

"Yes and yes," said Hakeem.

"It is against Islam!" the teacher declared.

"Why are you punishing my son for not reciting a Muslim prayer?" Hakeem asked. "Are beatings permissible?"

"Yes," the teacher said, "the principal and the parents agree I should."

Hakeem and his wife transferred their son to another school, and then another before they found one where Hussein experienced fewer attacks. Even as an eleven-year-old, Hussein remains steadfast in his faith: "I will never return to Islam, even if the persecution continues," he said. "Christ said we would suffer for him. It's okay to suffer for Christ, and we should be happy to suffer for him. The Lord is with me."

Even at his young age, Hussein knows that his goal is not to please man but to please God. "And I tell you, everyone who acknowledges me before men," Jesus taught, "the Son of Man also will acknowledge before the angels of God, but the one who denies me before men will be denied before the angels of God" (Luke 12:8–9).

Let us not forget our brothers and sisters—even children such as Hussein—who are persecuted for standing firm in their faith yet persevere. Will we stand with them in their suffering? Will we persevere with them in our prayers and in providing support for them?

26

A Modern-Day Job

John
Nigeria

In the village of Maseh in Nigeria's Plateau State, where farmland and gardens separate thatch-roof dwellings, Pastor John Ali Doro awoke and began preparing for the day. Pastor John filled various roles in life. He was leader of a small but committed group of Jesus followers. He was husband to a woman he loved. He was father to seven children and grandfather to a handful of boys and girls.

Life was good, but no pastor in Nigeria assumes such a role without accepting risk. Christians are the minority among the predominantly Muslim Fulani, an ethnic group that raises cattle in the region. The Fulani have increasingly become more radical and violent in their attacks against Christians. John knew that radical Islamic groups killed dozens of pastors.

Gunfire suddenly shattered the morning peace. Shouts of terror pierced the air. "The Fulani are coming!" someone yelled.

Pastor John dived into a nearby ditch to hide from the armed attackers. From a distance, he saw the Fulani zeroing in on the church. It was the largest building in the village, and people had run into it for safety. Flames soon burst through the windows. Helpless, Pastor John watched and listened in agony as dozens of his brothers and sisters in Christ—some members of his own family—wailed as they burned to death.

"Allahu akbar! Allahu akbar!" shouted the Fulani, the words meaning "God is great."

Then Pastor John heard one say, "Let's see if their God can save them now!"

After Nigerian Special Forces finally drove the attackers away, the smell of human flesh proved a prelude to the painful revelation inside. Forty-four people lay dead, including Pastor John's wife, four of his seven children, and two of his grandchildren.

The killing wasn't over.

The next day, at a mass funeral for those who died, the gunmen returned. They opened fire on the mourners. Among those killed were a national senator and a leader of the Plateau State House of Assembly. Pastor John learned that around ten other villages had been similarly attacked the previous day, leaving nearly two hundred people dead.

The common thread in the attacks? The targets were Christians.

At home, Pastor John tried unsuccessfully to make sense of the senselessness. It was impossible. Bitterness beckoned him, and his instinct was to hurt back. Instead, he made a choice.

"I just threw everything back to God," he said. "I prayed God would help the attackers understand that this is evil so that they can stop. I also asked God to help me to be able to use my life to propagate the gospel, because I knew that I could have died."

Instead of wishing evil on the attackers, he forgave the men who had killed his family and friends. He hopes they will receive salvation through Jesus. And although forgiveness brings healing, it does not erase sorrow and grief.

"It's painful," Pastor John said. "When they did all that and I lost my family, it was very painful. But there's nothing you can do to change the situation apart from lifting it to God." For encouragement to endure, he turned to the book of Job, the Bible's account of a man who had wave after tragic wave wash over him. "Job lost everything—wealth, children, everything but his wife," he said. "Yet he did not turn his back on God. That story has helped me, not only to deal with the situation, but even to remain who I am."

Pastor John related so closely to Job's story that he preached several sermons on it following the attack. "Job's wife told him to curse God and die," he said, "but his reply was that in the days where there is good from the Lord, we accept it. When there is difficulty, how can we refuse to accept that? Those thoughts encourage me and give me strength."

Adversity is unavoidable in life, but it does not necessitate defeat. The Word of God never promises Jesus followers a comfortable and secure life. It promises that, despite the inevitable storms of life, God is bigger than such storms. "In the world you will have tribulation. But take heart; I have overcome the world" (John 16:33).

Armed with the strength of God's Word, Pastor John continues to pray for those in his church family who lost loved ones during the attack. He continues to trust God and serve him.

"My request is that God should help me in my life as a Christian and as a pastor," he said, "to be able to do what God has called me to do well and to fulfill the purpose that God has for my life."

Perseverance is among the go-to tools God has placed in the toolbox of those who serve him. Perseverance tests us, steels us, and forms us into the people God wants us to be. Is this process easy? No. Just as sand on a beach results from the tumult of tides and waves, our character is shaped by the pain and difficulties we've endured for the cause of Jesus.

When trouble comes our way—and it will, as Pastor John knows so well—let's not run from it or retaliate. Let's trust in God and endure in faith, so we can fulfill the purpose God has for our lives.

27

It Started with a Soccer Game

Hassan S. and Pastor Hakim
Algeria

In 1983, a group of Algerian locals watched tourists set up their tents in the Tizi Ouzou Province one evening. "It was a windy place, and they set up the tents the wrong way," remembered Hassan, who was there with about a dozen friends. "The wind blew everything over—their tents and their belongings. We laughed at them and then went over to help."

One of the visitors expressed thanks for the help and then, in the spirit of friendship, extended an unusual invitation: "Would you do us the pleasure of engaging in a friendly soccer match tomorrow?"

Hassan huddled with his friends and replied, "We would love to, but our best player is sick in bed with a fever. Without him, we would probably not give you much of a game."

One of the visitors, his brow furrowed, asked, "This friend of yours—might we see him? We'd like to pray for his healing."

Now Hassan and his friends had furrowed brows. Prayer? Healing? God being interested in a single individual? These concepts seemed odd to the Algerians, yet they were intrigued by the offer.

So that night, the tourists prayed over the young man. In the morning, he felt no sign of sickness and played in the game. Amazed, the Algerians began asking questions about this apparent healing.

"Who is this 'Father' you prayed to who heals?" Hassan asked.

The tourists weren't missionaries. They were simply people who loved the Lord and were eager to share his glory. They explained the grace, salvation, and power offered through faith in Christ, then continued on with their journey. But in regard to Christianity, Algeria would not remain the same.

Algeria is an African country across the Mediterranean Sea from Spain. At one time, it was home to St. Augustine of Hippo, one of the most influential Christian scholars in history. But in more modern times, Christianity was nearly unknown. Before that soccer game, Algeria had no Christian bookstores, no functioning indigenous churches, and virtually no access to Bibles. The lone vestiges of Christian influence were abandoned churches left over from French colonialism, which ended in 1962. The few people attending church were generally foreign-born Catholics, who were allowed by law to practice their religion but forbidden to share it with the nation's Muslim population.

But after the tourists left, something "miraculous" started happening. "I felt that the stories they told were not just stories, but real," recalled Hassan. "It made me want to leave everything and follow Jesus." Hassan and other Algerians began turning to the God of the Bible. The "soccer miracle" is credited with initiating an explosion of faith in a country where Christians were once rare.

"We cannot count the number of people who came to Christ because of this," Hassan said. "We don't know how it happened, just that people came to faith and came to God."

In a short time, Christianity flourished and became the fastest-growing religion in Algeria. Pressured by hard-line Islamic nations, the Algerian government decided to curb the growth of Christianity and oppose followers of Jesus. Hassan and his friends were arrested time after time. But they and other believers would not be deterred. They remained faithful, and Christianity continued to spread.

Years—decades—passed, and Christianity remained a "problem" for radical Muslims. So in 2006, the Algerian parliament tightened restrictions on non-Islamic organizations. The passing of Ordinance 06-03 limited Christian worship to buildings that were registered with the government. The law also restricted non-Islamic literature and set criminal penalties for anyone who "incites, constrains or utilizes means of seduction tending to convert a Muslim to another religion" or who produces literature or videos that are designed to "shake the faith of Muslims." Violators face five years in prison and a thirteen-thousand-dollar fine.

In keeping with this ordinance, Algerian authorities closed twenty-six churches—buildings and house churches—in February 2008, claiming they were not registered. No new churches have been given government clearance since.

But God is in the miracle business. As one Algerian pastor said, "When God says he will continue his work, he will do that. We have a lot of problems, but each time we can see God's hand in the midst of trouble."

Shortly before the restrictions of Ordinance 06-03 went into effect, local authorities had granted a pastor a permit to build a new church in northern Algeria. Pastor Hakim was elated when he received the news. By 2009, more than three hundred people came to this church to worship—quite rare in a nation where 96 percent of the population is Muslim.

But Muslim extremists retaliated against Jesus followers violently and forcefully. In December 2009, more than twenty Muslims blocked the church entrance and prevented people from attending a Christmas service. Two days later, protesters broke into the building and stole microphones and speakers.

The next month, Muslims burst into a church service where they intimidated the congregation and threatened to kill Pastor Hakim. A week later, protesters stormed the church building and vandalized it until police arrived. Later, the protesters returned and burned the building to the ground, leaving a charred mess of Bibles, hymnals, and a cross.

The Christian community would not be deterred. They rebuilt the church. Again, Muslims extremists vandalized it. Again, the followers of Jesus persisted. When they were unable to perform baptisms in their church building, they baptized believers in kiddie pools and bathtubs in congregants' homes. No matter what obstacles they face, they remain committed to obeying Jesus in whatever way possible.

The Bible reminds us that difficulties are the default mode for Jesus followers. Accepting this, however, is not to admit defeat. As

Acts 14:21–22 says, "When they [Paul and Barnabas] had preached the gospel to that city and had made many disciples, they returned to Lystra and to Iconium and to Antioch, strengthening the souls of the disciples, encouraging them to continue in the faith, and saying that through many tribulations we must enter the kingdom of God." Believing this reality strengthens us as we persevere for the faith no matter where we live.

28

Making Good on Second Chances

Hussein A.

Iran

He was a drug addict. A leader of a counterfeiting ring. A familiar face to prostitutes. And as Hussein looked down from atop one of Tehran's hundreds of high-rises, he considered how he had once thought such activities would bring him happiness.

They didn't. Now, in his twenties, Hussein had decided his life was beyond salvaging.

The distant Elburz Mountains, coated in a fresh blanket of snow, rose up boldly to eighteen thousand feet. In contrast, Hussein felt quite small, insignificant, and unnoticed—merely a meaningless speck among the nearly ten million people in Iran's capital.

It is time, he thought, *to end my life*. But his plan to do so was proving problematic. He was afraid to jump, so he decided to buy a little of the drug Ecstasy to take the edge off. Just as he exited the building and reached the streets, his cell phone rang.

"I've found something new," an old army buddy and fellow addict said. "Meet me for tea."

Perfect timing, figured Hussein. *A new drug to steel my nerves for the final plunge.*

"Tell me about the stuff you found," Hussein said to his friend soon afterward, cold hands wrapped around a mug of tea. "I'm interested."

"Not *stuff*," said his friend. "Not drugs. Much better. Jesus!"

Hussein nearly spit out his tea. He looked around to make sure nobody had heard. *"What?"*

"I've found Jesus," he said in an excited whisper. "I've found peace. No more drugs. No more prostitutes. No more bullying people to make money."

Hussein was dumbfounded. But as his friend shared his story, something happened to Hussein: He stopped thinking about death. He stopped thinking about killing himself and started thinking about life.

Later, his friend had a Bible sent to Hussein and then introduced him to a group of Jesus followers who gathered in a local park on a sunny afternoon.

"I'd thought of killing myself too before I found Christ," said one of the women who heard Hussein's story. "Do you want to give all the pain in your life to Jesus?"

He could think of no reason why he wouldn't. *A God who wants a personal relationship with me? A God who speaks of loving others? A God who forgives sins—who will love me even if I make a mistake or miss a prayer?* So he received Jesus as his Savior and Lord.

"I still didn't understand what was happening to me," he recalled, "but I felt something was different. I knew my life was going to change. Christ just said he wanted me to be his son! This made me excited. This was very different from Islam. Immediately, I felt light, and I was unnecessarily happy for no reason."

He reveled in his newfound faith. Then came the testing, first by water and then by the authorities.

Hussein was at the beach, along the Caspian Sea, on a church retreat. He had never learned to swim, but egged on by his friends, he splashed in the waves with water rising up to his chest. Suddenly, he stepped off into deep water. Panicked, he thrashed and splashed, trying vainly to stay afloat. Then he began praying.

"Christ, give me one more chance," he prayed. Months earlier, he had sensed God calling him to ministry, but he had a good job, a house, and freedom, so he refused. Now he desperately longed to live, to have the opportunity to give up all he had for Jesus. "One more chance! I never ministered for you. I will minister for you if you do this. Just give me one more chance."

Several lifeguards dragged him from the depths. Time would show if his commitment had been born of true conviction or based only on a desperate will to live.

"You almost died," an Iranian church leader told Hussein after learning of his decision to be "all in" for Jesus. "You're feeling emotional right now. Do you know how hard it is to minister in Iran?"

"I don't care," Hussein said, sincere conviction in his voice. "I have to. Jesus gave me one more chance, and I have to do this. If I have to sacrifice everything I have, I will do this."

He quit his job, paid off his debts, and sold his car. Then he went into full-time ministry with a female coleader who ministered to women. As an evangelist, Hussein had a great combination: his story was compelling, his passion convincing, and his message convicting. "The favor of the Lord was with me," he said. "I felt God had anointed me to witness." Dozens of people came to profess faith in Christ through his ministry, but he would pay a price for these souls.

In the Kurdish area of Iran, Hussein became involved with a group that shipped Bibles into the country. One day, just after five hundred New Testaments arrived, eight members of the Iranian secret police rushed in. They did not show any search warrants; they just ravaged his apartment looking for Christian literature.

The police handcuffed Hussein, along with three female church leaders, and whisked them away in a van. While being taken to a prison, he was blindfolded and shackled, then transferred to another car. "This is just the beginning," one captor said smugly. "This is just the 'welcome parade.'"

Hussein prayed—not for himself, but that the small house church would not be destroyed. That the Bibles would not be captured. That their ministry would still find ways to keep proclaiming Jesus.

He was placed in solitary confinement, in a room the size of a large bathroom. There was no bed, toilet, or sink; just two floodlights, one of which was kept on 24-7 to mess with his mind.

Are the women safe? he worried. *Did they reveal names of church leaders who will now be in danger? How can I warn them? Have the police discovered the Bibles?*

"Let's pray together."

These words came out of nowhere—amid dead silence in a room where he was the only person, and he was not talking.

Hussein believes they were the words of Jesus: "I felt like Jesus put everything aside—the whole world aside—to come whisper in my ear. He said to me, 'There is no need for you to say anything because I am going to tell you what to say. Why are you afraid? At the end you are going to die, right? So why don't you just serve? Don't you have faith that when you close your eyes in this world, you will open them up to me? And when you open your eyes, you will be in my arms?'"

Hussein's interrogations began the next day. Whenever he answered a question in a way the interrogators did not like, they kicked him in the stomach. After three days, he was taken to court to face an apostasy charge, which in Iran could carry the death penalty.

"Why do you have a problem with mosques and imams?" a judge asked. "Why do you want to destroy Islam?"

Hussein was taken back to the main prison. He actually missed solitary confinement where he could pray to God without all the distractions.

"Only God can help you in here," a guard told him.

"Yes," said Hussein, "he *is* helping me."

Hussein was assigned to death row, where 250 inmates obeyed gang leaders instead of guards. Hussein prayed harder. That night, the gang leaders told Hussein to meet them at midnight in the bathroom. Instead of hurting him, however, they asked for his help. Did he have information about his prison friends in America?

Is there some mistake? Do they think I am someone else? Hussein had no prison friends in America, but the gang leaders believed otherwise and gave him first-class treatment because of it. He got the top bunk and a private shower. He was given fresh vegetables.

After two days, when the guards offered to transfer him to a "safer" part of the prison, Hussein stunned them when he declined.

Eight days later, his family brought the deed to his house as collateral and Hussein was released on bail. During his hearing, the judge pointed out some mistakes in his appeal document and personally corrected them. "Here," he said, slipping Hussein a piece of paper. "This is my cell phone number. I'll personally supervise your case. And to make it more convenient for you, I won't require you to make the four-hour trip to the courthouse."

Again, Hussein was amazed by how God had intervened.

The five hundred Bibles that Hussein prayed would be kept safe were never discovered by the police, even though they were in boxes in the middle of the living room.

He could only shake his head and praise God. "It was like when Paul was in jail and an earthquake opened the doors," he said. "Look how many doors God opened for me! This is why I want to keep serving, because I know God is with me."

How does he see his future? The light of God has penetrated his darkest moments when he thought his life was over. With a grateful heart, he is determined to continue serving God with the "one chance" he asked Jesus to give him. "They will either kill me, or there will be other miraculous events like these," he said. "Which one is bad?"

29

Anything to Do God's "Big Work"

Ruth and Armando
The Philippines

Rather than surrender to Islamist killers, Ruth, her husband, Armando, and their three children ran through the darkness to hide under a footbridge. For hours, they huddled in shallow canal water frequented by poisonous snakes. It was the only place that could conceal them.

The family was surprised when they first heard the percussion of bombs and the crack of rifles shatter the night's silence. Mindanao, an island region of the Philippines, had experienced conflict since 2000 when President Joseph Estrada's "All Out War" declaration pitted government troops against Islamist groups seeking to establish an independent Islamic state. Four out of ten households—nearly a million people—had been displaced by the conflict.

But Ruth and Armando's family had experienced no vestiges of violence since they moved to their village in central Mindanao in 1990. In the Philippines, about three times as many people practice

Christianity as Islam. In the village where they lived, the population was evenly split between Muslims and Christians, and the couple had come to establish a church there.

Now violent Islamist fighters had slipped silently through the dark jungle thick with bamboo, ferns, and banana trees and attacked the village of about eight hundred sleeping people. The family's fear of the attacking fighters was rivaled only by that of the typhoons that also swept across the island with no regard for the devastation left behind.

Ruth whispered to her frightened children, "You must be quiet. Very, very quiet."

That proved difficult for children who had little idea what being caught might mean. They cried. For eight hours, Ruth and Armando whispered encouragement to their children and prayed for protection for their family and ministry.

The next morning, they crawled out of their hiding place and hurriedly gathered a few essential belongings before disappearing into the jungle with other villagers who had survived the attack. Nightfall, they knew, would bring more fighting. For several weeks, they camped in the jungle in makeshift tents made using sheets, tarps, rice-drying sacks—whatever they had.

During the next five years, the family occasionally had to flee just as they had the first time the rebels attacked. Rebel forces attacked the village twice in 2009, killing four Jesus followers and leaving more than two hundred people homeless. Another time they kidnapped several villagers to use as human shields.

In fact, rebels were so often near the village that residents adopted a new routine. They would stay in the village and tend livestock and gardens during the day; every night they would leave to sleep in makeshift tents. Through all the hardship and risk, Ruth and Armando stayed to raise their children and to remain faithful to the work God had for them.

After their children grew up and enrolled in college, Ruth and Armando could have easily left. Yet they didn't. They saw the hand of God at work and chose to continue their task for his glory.

"For I consider that the sufferings of this present time," Paul wrote, "are not worth comparing with the glory that is to be revealed to us.... And we know that for those who love God all things work together for good, for those who are called according to his purpose" (Romans 8:18, 28).

Each day, Ruth and Armando persevere by choosing to focus their attention on the hope of Christ rather than the hardships of life. It is a practice they have not only learned but also taught. One of their daughters is studying at a theology school and plans to return to Mindanao to help in her parents' ministry.

"I thank God because she is willing," Ruth said. "There is a big work in this place. Let us continue to serve the Lord even though we are experiencing this kind of persecution. All these things are happening to us, but God is still great … God has called us here. If we die, we *die*."

30

Rolling On amid the Resistance

Walid
Iraq and Lebanon

Walid rolled his wheelchair to his car and, with help from a companion, slipped into the driver's seat. Yes, it would be easier to stay at home. It would be easier to just sit and watch television. It would be easier not to take a single risk. It was risk, after all, that had cost him the use of his legs.

"But," Walid asked, "how would God be served by that?"

Lives needed to be saved for eternity. He had Bibles to pass out. He needed to make new connections with nonbelievers. So he turned the key and, thanks to hands-only controls, carried on with his work for the Lord in the Middle East.

"We all have our crosses to bear," he said. "I'm happy to bear this cross for the Lord."

Walid had grown up in Mosul, Iraq. After becoming a Christian, he moved to Lebanon to serve a church there. Ironically, church leaders believed it best for him to return to Mosul and plant churches.

For a missionary, being sent to Mosul was like a soldier being sent to the front lines. He welcomed the challenge.

The desert environment of northern Iraq is considered to be the Cradle of Civilization. Historic figures of the Old Testament—Abraham, Daniel, Esther, and Jonah—spent time there. Christians have lived there for more than two thousand years. But since 2003, more than a million Christians have fled Iraq.

The mass exodus and the risks that caused it didn't deter Walid. He found an apartment in Mosul, connected with a community of believers, and began sharing the gospel with Muslims.

Unlike the stadium-based evangelism often seen in the West, Walid's approach is more like guerrilla warfare. He makes progress one conversation at a time. He shares the Word quietly, almost like a spy who has information to pass on but must do so undetected.

The chaos in Iraq has made Muslims increasingly open to Christ. Hundreds of thousands of Iraqis have died. Confronted with the possibility of death, they long for peace, joy, and assurance—hope they aren't finding in Islam. Many are seeking answers about the God of the Bible.

Walid's house church grew quickly. A handful of people became a dozen, then two dozen. Within five months, sixty people were part of the church. In a place like Mosul, the tragic and sometimes deadly irony is that the more "successful" a church is, the greater the chance its members will be persecuted. Walid was certainly aware of what could happen, but it did not deter him.

"What is it, Walid?" his mother asked while riding in the passenger seat next to him. "You saw something in the mirror, no? Are we being followed?"

Walid glanced in his rearview mirror again and then toward his mother. "We're fine," he assured her.

"You cannot fool a mother," she replied.

"Perhaps he thinks we are someone else."

Then the car behind them accelerated suddenly. Walid stepped on the gas too, but the pursuing car was too fast. Within seconds, it pulled alongside. Oncoming traffic swerved out of the way, kicking up dirt and rocks.

Walid was locked in panic, trying amid the chaos to protect his mother, avoid the other car, and not run into oncoming cars.

Pffft! Pffft! Pffft!

He felt the sting of a bullet in his back but managed to ease the car to the side of the road. As the assailant's car sped away, Walid felt as if he were going to black out.

"Mother, are you okay?" he managed to say. "Were you hit?"

He heard no answer.

Days later, at the hospital, his blurred vision sharpened. He could see his mother's face. She sat at his bedside, and a doctor explained what had happened.

"One bullet went through both of you," he said. "Walid, I am sorry. It hit your spinal cord. You will likely never walk again."

It was difficult news—very tough to deal with.

"But your mother," said the doctor, "was lucky. She was struck only in the arm."

When visitors came, Walid never talked about himself. He spoke about how happy he was that his mother was not injured more severely. He shared how burdened he was for other evangelists in Iraq.

"They are carrying a bigger and heavier cross than most Christians," he said. "And despite the difficult situation, the salvation of souls is taking place in big numbers in Iraq. Pray that the Lord will intervene directly to strengthen, encourage, and empower us to do his work so that we can bring truth to Iraq."

Then he gripped the wheels of his chair, as if nothing had happened, and began rolling forward for God's glory. Walid is a great example for us of 1 Thessalonians 3:7–8: "For this reason, brothers, in all our distress and affliction we have been comforted about you through your faith. For now we live, if you are standing fast in the Lord."

Walid perseveres regardless of the obstacles in his way. He knows he serves a God who will sustain his children through every kind of challenge. Walid reminds us that standing fast has absolutely nothing to do with our physical capabilities and everything to do with our resolve to hold firmly to God's promises, regardless of our circumstances.

Martyrs in History

John Bradford
1510–1555
England

Though you are in the world yet you are not of the world. You
are not of them which look for their portion in this life.... You
are of them that know yourselves to be ... pilgrims and strangers;
for here you have no dwelling-place. You are of them whose
portion is the Lord, and which have their hope in heaven.

John Bradford, *The Patient Suffering of Trouble and Affliction for Christ's Cause*

Sixteenth-century England was a dangerous time and place to be an
outspoken believer in Christ. While many people "changed colors"
during that time to avoid death, John Bradford stayed true to Christ.
It cost him a promising career in government, and in 1555, it cost
him his life.

Born into a wealthy family and with training in business and
law, Bradford found service in the government of the notorious King
Henry VIII. The king's desire for an heir compelled him to break

from the Roman Church, which would play a significant role in Bradford's future.

While Bradford was a law student in London, he committed his life to Christ. He then studied theology and was ordained a chaplain at Cambridge in 1550. At that time, he witnessed a column of prisoners being led to their execution and commented, "There but for the grace of God goes John Bradford." The common modification of that phrase, "There but for the grace of God go I," is still used today.

When the Church of England was first established as a Protestant body, Bradford emerged as a fiery Protestant who rebuked nobles for their "insatiable covetousness," "filthy carnality," "intolerable ambition and pride," and unwillingness to attend to "poor men's causes and to hear God's Word."

Not surprisingly, many people hated him. But he persevered in sharing his Bible-based beliefs. His fortune changed dramatically when young King Edward VI died and Mary Tudor came to the throne. She desperately wanted England to return to the Catholic Church. To that end, she had Bradford arrested and tried for heresy. She condemned more than three hundred martyrs, Bradford among them, earning her reputation as "Bloody Mary."

Prior to his execution, Bradford was imprisoned for two years in a dank English cell. He was so favored and trusted by the guards that they allowed him to leave some evenings, knowing he would return by morning. He always did.

Bradford reminded Jesus followers that they weren't of this world. He reminded them of the glory in being "beaten, buffeted, scourged, crowned with thorns, banged upon the cross and utterly left by all his disciples." He encouraged believers not to be worn down by those who opposed Christ.

"Is it not written," Bradford emphasized, "who shall separate us from the love of God? Shall tribulation, or anguish, or persecution, or hunger, or nakedness, or peril, or sword? As it is written, 'For thy sake are we killed all the day long, and are counted as sheep appointed to be slain.'"

When he was examined by a church court convened to determine fault, Bradford was asked if he would accept the queen's mercy. "I shall be glad of the queen's favor on terms that correspond with my duty to Him whose favor is life, but whose displeasure is worse than any death mortals can inflict."

He was led to the stake on July 1, 1555. Bradford asked forgiveness of any he had wronged and granted forgiveness to the soldiers around him. He then picked up a stick and kissed it. He was bound to the stake with a younger prisoner, who heard from Bradford this assurance as flames lifted around them: "Brother, be of good comfort, for we shall have a mercy supper with the Lord this night, where all our pains will end in peace, and our warfare in songs of joy."

Part V

FORGIVENESS

*Bearing with one another and, if one has a complaint
against another, forgiving each other; as the Lord
has forgiven you, so you also must forgive.*

Colossians 3:13

Stories of Jesus followers who are hated and violently persecuted because of their faith have a powerful impact. It can be overwhelming to consider the suffering, pain, and grief they endure. Yet even more compelling than stories of their faithful perseverance under persecution are stories of their forgiveness for those who persecute them.

Forgiveness? Sincere forgiveness for the people who hate and harm them? Yes!

Among their stories are those of a mother who forgives the soldier who raped and killed her daughter, a teenager who forgives the men who burned down the village church with her family members inside, a woman who forgives the man who continues to torture her husband because he led a Bible study for Muslims curious about its teachings.

When such deep and sincere forgiveness is offered, it surprises us. It catches us off guard because forgiving those who persecute us is a distinctly supernatural act. Forgiveness for atrocities and murder committed against our loved ones is an abnormal human response.

Yet Jesus commands his followers to do what is humanly abnormal. We are to bless people who abuse us. We are to love our enemies. And we are to forgive with the love and compassion Jesus expressed as he died on the cross, praying, "Father, forgive them, for they know not what they do" (Luke 23:34).

How is it possible to do this? The path toward forgiveness is not easy, and forgiveness doesn't erase the painful consequences of evil in life. Are our persecuted brothers and sisters in Christ endowed with superhuman powers that make them eager to forgive those who perpetuate evil against them? No. Do they rationalize what has happened to them so it is easier to deny and avoid their pain? No. Are they in some ways immune to the sinfulness of the human heart that drives us to anger, bitterness, revenge, and retaliation? No.

They are people who struggle to forgive just as we do. The only difference is that they make the choice, in faith, to obey God. "Since God tells us in his Word to forgive," they say, "we must do it."

Forgiveness is simply an obedient response to God, who graciously forgives and in Jesus has provided us an example to follow. There is no magic formula for generating a sincere desire to forgive. Nothing less than the power of a trusting relationship with God can nurture forgiveness in a wounded heart.

As our persecuted brothers and sisters in Christ say yes to God and study the Bible, pray, and seek to mature in their relationship with him, God accomplishes a miracle in their hearts and minds.

Their walk with him deepens. They begin to see their abusers through God's eyes. They learn to forgive! When deep trauma has occurred, it may take a long time for that transformation to take place. But God is patient, kind, and faithful to accomplish his good work in the hearts of all those who seek, trust, and obey him.

31

Allowing God to Handle Everything

Danjuma
Nigeria

At 6:00 a.m. on that terrible day, gunshots jolted Danjuma awake. Like everyone else in his small village, Danjuma ran for his life. But the pungent smoke from houses set on fire choked him, and escape from the attack by nearly one thousand Islamic insurgents proved impossible for the thirteen-year-old boy.

Danjuma remembers all too well the pain of a machete slicing through the left side of his head. But he recalls nothing, thankfully, of what happened next. Not the machete blows to his left arm. Not the gouging out of his eye with a knife. Not the cutting off of his genitals. He only vaguely remembers the disbelief and excitement of the men who had been digging his grave when they realized he was still alive.

Twenty-three Nigerian Christians died that day. Thirty-eight were injured. The staff at the hospital fifteen miles away where Danjuma was taken could not believe he was among the survivors.

"They were astonished that this boy would come back alive after all of this," said Hadilia Adamu, a hospital manager. "He bled so much. It is a miracle."

Now Danjuma has the nickname "Miracle," not only because he lived, but also because he did not choose the path of bitterness. He feels less sorry for himself than for those who maimed him. "I forgive them because they don't know what they are doing," he said, echoing words he had read in the Bible. "If they had love, they wouldn't behave that way."

His forgiving attitude and abiding joy provide a powerful example to us. His story reminds us of God's desire for all who follow him to forgive and live in peace. In that sense, Danjuma brings to mind Isaiah 11:6: "The wolf shall dwell with the lamb, and the leopard shall lie down with the young goat, and the calf and the lion and the fattened calf together; and a little child shall lead them."

Danjuma, the boy with the peaceful smile, truly leads us in living out the words of Jesus each and every day: "But I say to you, love your enemies and pray for those who persecute you" (Matthew 5:44).

When we face injustice or injury at the hands of others, it is so easy for bitterness to become rooted in our lives. In contrast, Danjuma's commitment to avoid all the destructive attitudes a person could justify after being maimed and nearly murdered is something each of us needs to take to heart. It is something he continues to seek God's help in and asks for prayers toward that end. There is great hope in forgiving, in being free to say, as Danjuma did after leaving the hospital, "So there is no problem.

God continues to guide and protect. I have allowed God to handle everything."

May we pray faithfully for the Danjumas of the world who bear on their bodies the marks of Jesus (Galatians 6:17), that God will bless them and sustain them. May we pray that we, too, will choose to face our hardships and trials with forgiving hearts, trusting God to handle whatever we may experience.

32

Point-Blank Forgiveness

Habila Adamu
Nigeria

During a hot and humid night in northern Nigeria, quiet descended on the village where Habila Adamu and his family slept in their concrete-block house. At precisely 11:00 p.m., according to his clock, someone pounded on his door.

"Come out!" a man shouted. "And bring your family too!"

Habila threw on clothes and gathered his wife, Vivian, and their young son. When he opened the door, intruders clad in robes and masks greeted him. His fear deepened. One man brandished an AK-47.

The lead man nodded his head in a cocky manner. "We are here to do the work of Allah."

Too stunned to say anything, Habila knew that his words weren't nearly as important as the prayer he silently uttered: *Father, your will be done.*

The man asked Habila his name, where he worked, and whether he was a police officer or member of the military. Then he asked what proved to be the most important question: "Are you a Christian or Muslim?"

Habila did not hesitate. "I am a Christian."

Terror contorted Vivian's face. She knew these men were members of Boko Haram, a jihadist group responsible for the deaths of about ten thousand Nigerian citizens in 2014 alone.

"We are offering you a better life," one man stated, "if you will only say the *shahada*." The *shahada* is the Islamic profession of faith. The man taunted, "Go ahead, say it: 'There is no god but Allah, and Muhammad is his messenger.' Say it. Join us. Become a Muslim and join Boko Haram."

Habila glanced at his wife and son. "I am a Christian—and will always remain a Christian—even to death."

A man turned his attention to Vivian and offered a disingenuous smile. "If your husband does not cooperate, you will watch him die."

Vivian began to cry.

"A second chance, Mr. Adamu. Say the *shahada*."

Habila remained silent.

"Your husband," said the intruder, "is stubborn. Why can't you convince him to deny Christ and live a good life?" He raised the barrel of the rifle to Habila's head.

"Do not worry," Habila told his wife. "The death of a Christian is a great gain, not a loss."

"Bring me all the money you have," the man declared to Vivian, no longer smiling. "Now!"

She scoured the rooms of their small home, grabbing anything of value that might convince these men to leave. The intruder was not impressed. He lowered the barrel to Habila's mouth. "Since you refuse to become a Muslim," he said, "here is your reward."

Blam! The bullet passed through Habila's mouth. He fell to the floor and lay still, blood pouring out. Horrified, Vivian screamed. Their little boy burst into tears.

"Shut up, woman!" an attacker yelled. "If you try to get help, we will find you and kill you—and your child."

One man kicked Habila's leg to make sure he was dead. Satisfied that they had appeased Allah, they chanted, *"Allahu akbar,"* and left.

Vivian bent down to the man she loved. "I ... am ... still ... alive," Habila whispered, straining. "Please ... get help."

Vivian raced to a neighbor who had a phone and called the police. They did not come. Finally, Vivian and her neighbors got Habila to a hospital at 6:00 a.m.

"It is only by God's grace that he survived," said a doctor.

Medical personnel scheduled Habila to undergo a bone graft to repair his cheekbone. Before the doctors began the operation, however, they were stunned to see that his cheekbone had virtually healed! The graft was unnecessary.

Once Habila recovered and returned home, he eagerly began sharing his story. Nearly every time he tells it, listeners ask the obvious question: "And how do you feel about the men who did this to you?"

Instead of talking about them, Habila speaks of forgiveness. "We are all condemned criminals," he tells them. "Jesus died for us. He loves us. That's why we must show that love to the people who hate us."

And that is why Habila has prayed the same prayer every day since the night he was shot. Echoing the words of Jesus as he hung on the cross, Habila prays, "God, forgive them. God, forgive them."

He prays earnestly that the men who came that night will find the same peace in Christ that he has. "I love them," he says. "If I have the opportunity to see them, I will hug them and I will pray for them."

"But how can you do that—forgive the people who nearly killed you, who nearly robbed your family of a husband and a father?" he is sometimes asked.

"Because," he replies, "Christ is love. The God I am serving is love. And he commands us to love one another."

33

We Will Leave You in Peace

Jamil
Central Asia

As he had done nearly every night for three years, Jamil bent over the sink and washed the blood off his face. It was, he believed, a small price to pay for being hated because he loved and proclaimed Jesus. But soon he would reach a breaking point.

Jamil had been raised in a moderate Muslim family in Central Asia, in an area south of Russia, north of Iran and Afghanistan. At one point, his brother had adopted such radical beliefs that he was put in prison. For Jamil, that event triggered deep soul searching.

He searched diligently for spiritual truth. Through his studies, he met Christians who shared the gospel with him. Jesus, he realized, was all that Allah was not. The one true God. The promised one. The Savior.

He accepted Jesus with gusto and began sharing his faith as if he were a dying man who had found water in the desert and wanted to give it to everyone who was thirsty. And people he met were thirsty for the gospel. He led his brother, a former Islamic extremist, to

Christ. He led three other siblings to Christ. He planted four house churches.

After getting married and then fathering a son, he accepted an offer to be a missionary in another part of Central Asia. He moved his family to a village comprised entirely of Muslims. When word spread of this Jesus follower, this *kafir*, the nightly beatings began.

Each time, Jamil refused to retaliate. Instead, he shared Scripture verses with his attackers. But one night the beatings went too far. A lone man had come to beat him. As Jamil endured the punches, his six-year-old son walked into the room. The attacker thrust his fist into the little boy's stomach. The boy crumpled to the floor, writhing in pain.

Instinctively, Jamil rushed to protect his child. Jamil's turn-the-other-cheek spirit gave way to an adrenaline-fueled lust for revenge. When the attacker fled, Jamil found a knife and raced into the night after him.

When he burst into the home where the man lived, the man's elderly father was sitting in the front room.

"Where is your son?" demanded Jamil, breathless, his eyes like those of a madman. "I am going to *kill* him!"

"Jamil, this isn't like you," the man replied. "Why do you want to kill my son?"

"I can take the beatings," he answered. "I cannot take the beating of my son, which is what your son just did."

Momentarily deterred by a man who, like him, loved his son and did not want to see him hurt, Jamil ran on through the village. Everywhere he went, he spewed threats of revenge to anyone who would listen—and to some who wouldn't.

"Anyone who touches my son," he promised, "I will *kill*."

When Jamil returned home that night, he could not sleep. It wasn't just the attack on his son that troubled him. It was the guilt he felt for sinking as low as his attacker and vowing to extract justice by using violence. He knew what he had to do.

Before the sun rose, he walked to the home of the man who had attacked his son. Although the son and his father feared retaliation, Jamil had not come for revenge.

"I am sorry for my threat," he said humbly. "I do not want to kill you. I do not want to kill anyone. Please forgive me."

Despite his appeal for forgiveness, the nightly beatings continued. One night the leaders of the local Islamist group were about to leave on a hunting trip. They barged into Jamil's home to beat him and then turned to his wife.

"You," one man demanded, "cook for us."

The men took their places around the table as if daring her to refuse. Jamil's wife looked at her husband, uncertain how to respond.

"Please," he said, "cook for them."

So she prepared a meal for the men who sat at her table, the same men who routinely beat her husband. As the men waited, Jamil said, "It does not matter how cruel you have been to me or to anyone else. God will forgive you and accept you into his kingdom if you repent and place your faith in Christ." He then paused. "May God bless your hunt."

The men looked at him, and then at each other, in disbelief.

"We came here to eat your food and to beat you," stated the leader, "but now we cannot." He looked at the others and continued. "We will leave you in peace."

Days later, the leader invited Jamil to his home. "Please," he said, "share with my family what you shared with us the other night."

It was the first time one of his tormentors asked to learn about Christ, and it would not be the last.

God's message of love and forgiveness is available to all people, as affirmed in John 3:16: "For God so loved the world, that he gave his only Son, that whoever believes in him should not perish but have eternal life." The bold love of God can reach our enemies. It is powerful enough to melt even the hardest heart. His forgiveness transforms the coldest heart.

We cannot change those around us in our own strength. But the Holy Spirit within us can disarm the most vicious people as we faithfully demonstrate God's love and forgiveness. What finally allowed Jamil the opportunity to share God's love with these hateful men was forgiveness and bold love. It certainly isn't easy for a father to forgive someone who intentionally injures his young child. It isn't easy for a woman to cook dinner for the men who beat her husband and son. And it isn't easy to bless those who hate us. But that is the path of forgiveness.

Let us pray diligently for our persecuted brothers and sisters who suffer so much in the battle against evil. Pray that those who fight against the faithful will see God's love and forgiveness in action and realize that he provides another way. Pray that they will be set free from their bondage to hatred and evil.

34

Continue to Love the Muslims

Mousa Tinibu
Niger

Pastor Mousa Tinibu raced through his village in Niger's Zinder Province as if he were a hunted animal. So did the others from his church—women in colorful dresses and men in flowing shirts.

Panic drove them past thatch-roof houses. Fields of parched crops. Granaries that rose from the ground like giant peanuts. Donkeys, camels, and everything else that made their village home.

They ran from death.

In the panic and confusion, Pastor Tinibu tried to make sense of a senseless situation. *Why, in our own village, are our neighbors trying to kill us?*

Gunshots rang out. People screamed. Children cried.

"Hurry up!" someone near him yelled. "They are still chasing us!"

It was January 17, 2015. The previous day, Muslim protests had erupted in French-speaking Niger after a controversial cartoon depicting the prophet Muhammad appeared on the cover of the satirical magazine *Charlie Hebdo*. Now Christians—every Christian—had become a target for angry Muslims.

"We were overwhelmed," the pastor said, "because we knew this was in the Bible, but we had never tasted it for ourselves."

What stunned him and other believers was that the Republic of Niger was not like other countries in this part of the world where Christianity was, and is still, not accepted by law. People in Niger are free to change their religious identity, and Christians are permitted to build churches and schools. Evangelical Christians are hardly a threat. They comprise only .1 percent of the population in a country of 18 million residents where 94 percent are Muslim. But now, in the eyes of their pursuers, Jesus followers were the enemy.

"We were just blown away because here we are in our village, with our own families and with people who have benefited from a Christian presence in this town, and now we were being chased," Pastor Tinibu said later. Then he realized the flip side to the madness. "The Lord encouraged us. When we were overwhelmed, the Lord reminded us that we are worthy—worthy to suffer shame for his name."

And suffer they did.

By the end of the day, attacks in Zinder and the capital city of Niamey left ten people dead and 170 injured. More than seventy churches were destroyed, along with numerous Christian schools, organizations, and orphanages. More than one hundred houses belonging to pastors were looted or destroyed.

Even more would have died if the gendarmerie, a military force tasked with policing the village, had not allowed fleeing Christians to climb aboard their trucks and whisked them from harm's way.

The next day, Pastor Tinibu and his congregation were stunned as they saw that fire had gutted their church. At first, it seemed that they had lost everything. But during the weeks to come, as he saw how his people responded to the devastation, this Bible verse came to mind: "Blessed are you when others revile you and persecute you and utter all kinds of evil against you falsely on my account. Rejoice and be glad, for your reward is great in heaven, for so they persecuted the prophets who were before you" (Matthew 5:11–12).

Amid the mourning, Pastor Tinibu saw a wisp of hope take root, like a sapling sprouting from bone-dry soil. Prior to the attack, he had noted that people attending the church seemed preoccupied with their own lives. Now they became more involved in visiting and caring for one another. A deeper level of community emerged in the church, and the rest of the village noticed.

What's more, those who followed Jesus experienced a deeper level of forgiveness. "God is encouraging us to continue to love the Muslims despite what happened," the pastor said. "It's not easy, but he wants us to forgive and to love because we have met Muslims who truly regret what they did and what happened."

Similar attacks have continued as a radical branch of Islam deepens its roots in West Africa. But Pastor Tinibu and people in the church stand strong in their Christ-based convictions. "There is a great reward that awaits us," he said, "and one of the benefits of this great reward is suffering."

In the midst of that suffering, Christians have the privilege of sharing God's gift of forgiveness with others. One Muslim woman who ran with Pastor Tinibu and the others to the gendarmerie that day couldn't help but notice the Christians' unwillingness to seek revenge against their attackers—or even to seethe in bitterness. She also couldn't help but notice the lust for blood that had driven some Muslims to kill. She accepted Jesus as her Savior.

We serve a God who loves and forgives. He sends us out "as lambs in the midst of wolves" (Luke 10:3). Let us support one another in being Christ's witnesses who love and forgive others—even those who mean us harm.

35

The Possibilities of Forgiveness

Pauline Ayyad
Gaza City

In terms of dangerous professions, managing a bookstore wouldn't seem to be on the list of high-risk occupations. Certainly, being a logger, deep-sea fisherman, or high-rise window washer would be dangerous. But a bookstore manager? No. Unless it is a Christian bookstore in a place where some view the Christian faith as a threat and react violently to it.

Rami Ayyad ran a Christian bookstore for the Palestinian Bible Society in Gaza City, a Muslim-dominated city of half a million people in the Gaza Strip. The store served about thirty-five hundred Palestinian Christians who lived in Gaza City, most of whom belonged to the Greek Orthodox, Roman Catholic, or Baptist denominations. In Hamas territory, individuals sometimes pay a high price for identifying with such groups. That was what made Rami's work dangerous.

Pauline Ayyad, a young mother of two with a third child on the way, knew extremists had their eyes on the bookstore. They threatened it regularly. They had bombed it twice. But her husband, Rami, remained steadfast in his belief that he was doing the right thing by working there.

"Jesus is the love of my life," he told her, "and I will never deny him, regardless of what happens."

In October 2007, three men showed up at the bookstore. "They are fundamentalists with long beards," her husband said during a panicked phone call before they kidnapped him. Those were the last words Pauline ever heard her husband speak. Early the next morning, his body was found near the store—scarred with bullet holes and knife wounds.

Upon learning of her husband's death, anger stabbed Pauline as if she, too, had been stabbed and shot to death. And the pain wouldn't go away. "What good is going to come out of this?" she asked the Lord. "What good could come to me after the death of my husband?"

For a time, she said she "hated Muslims, hated everybody." But when reading Ecclesiastes 3, she began to understand that God's plans aren't always our plans. She realized that in life there is a time for everything, even dark things like death: "a time to be born, and a time to die" (3:2).

"That was the beginning of my forgiveness journey," she said. But only the beginning.

"I forgave them, but very much on the surface," she recounted later. "I wasn't *really* forgiving them."

The Bible Society moved her to Bethlehem, where they believed she and her children would be safer. As she received support, encouragement, and prayer from Jesus followers around the world, she struggled with her feelings toward her husband's killers. Then, five years after his death, she attended a conference where a key truth bore through to her soul for the first time: the Muslims who killed her husband were the very ones she and other Christians needed to reach for Jesus.

"I felt like a totally different person," she remembered. "I felt I had a new spirit, a new heart, and a new mind full of forgiveness and acceptance of the situation that the Lord allowed in my life."

Pauline became involved in outreach to Muslim women in her Bethlehem community. She opened a small gift shop near the Church of the Nativity in order to help support her family. Perhaps more important, she realized something she hadn't considered earlier.

"Six years after Rami's death, I discovered what a great honor it is to be the widow of a martyr," she said. "For my family and me, Jesus became a reality, meeting our needs like a husband, a father, a helper. He became everything—the person I could rely on."

She now encourages widows with the message that took her so long to learn: "Don't bury yourself with your husband. No, go outside and be a testimony. Experience Jesus and let him lift you up and use you in miraculous ways to bring glory and honor to his name."

Losing a loved one always hurts; that pain is a testament to how much that person meant to us. But bitterness in the heart is like swallowing poison and expecting the person who wounded us to die. When Pauline was able to truly forgive her husband's killers, she was set free from bitterness, which opened her life to new possibilities.

The catalyst for Pauline was not only *saying* she forgave her husband's killers but also *being certain in her soul* that she had forgiven them. Once she allowed God to wash away her bitterness, she was free to begin living an abundant life for his glory.

36

Face to Face with Her Assailant

Amina

Nigeria

In the northern Nigerian village of Kataru, darkness mirrored the evil that lurked in the early morning quiet. As she lay in bed in her mud-walled house that April morning, Amina Yakubu was awakened by a slight tug in her abdomen. *Ah, just the baby kicking again.* Six-months pregnant with their third child, she drifted back to sleep. Her husband was away hunting.

Ch-ch-ch-ch-ch-ch-ch-ch-ch-ch-ch-ch-ch-ch.

Amina bolted upright. *Machine-gun fire?* She called to her friend who was staying in the adjacent room. "Get the children! Fulani!"

A year earlier, Fulani warriors, Islamic terrorists who hate Christians, massacred more than five hundred men, women, and children in a nearby village. Amina never thought it would happen in their village. But just in case, she had created a secret hiding place for the children.

She and her friend threw on some clothes and gathered the half-asleep children. She quickly patted her abdomen. "It's okay, baby. It's—"

A noise outside the house ramped up her fear.

"Out the back," she whispered to her friend. "Over the fence. I'll go first. Hand me the children."

"God, help us," she prayed as she tried to get her pregnant body over the fence. Partway up, her leg exploded in pain from a bullet. She dropped back to the ground, narrowly missing a child.

Leaving a bloody trail, her friend dragged Amina back to the house with kids in tow. She locked the door and shuffled the children into the hiding place.

Seconds later, the door flew open. A Fulani warrior raised a machete above his head. Amina raised a hand to block the blow, but he sliced the blade into her scalp, neck, and arms. She slumped to the floor, left for dead in a pool of blood. Not finding anyone else in the house, he left to help set fire to the village.

Hours later, Amina awoke in a hospital, transported there by a Nigerian army crew. Her baby was delivered stillborn. It took doctors a very long time to suture all her wounds. It took even longer for her to stop sobbing.

As her husband visited with her, Amina mourned the loss of her baby and lamented the pain she felt.

"Those who did this to you," her husband asked, "if the army brings them to you and you see them, what will you say should be done to them?"

Amina paused. Even speaking was difficult. "Do to them … what they … did to … me."

He looked away and then into her eyes. "You won't forgive them?"

"I will … never … forgive them," she whispered.

Weeks passed in the hospital. Weeks to reflect. Weeks to pray. Weeks to consider God's will, not hers.

Then her husband asked the question again.

"If I see those who attacked me, if they are arrested and brought to me, I have forgiven them," she replied. "All this suffering I am going through, even before it happened, I know that the Lord had already known and he has written it, that at so-and-so time I will find myself in this suffering. Therefore, I will forgive them."

Four months later, she was discharged from the hospital. Four months after that, she was at her mother's house when a man came to deliver firewood. Their eyes met. It was the man who had attacked her. She knew it. He knew it.

"When I looked up and saw him, my heart just split open," Amina said. "I started thinking of all that had happened to me."

The man looked everywhere but at her. He put the wood down, received his pay from her mother, and left.

Her uncle later chastised her for not speaking up. He wasn't interested in her telling the man she had forgiven him. He wanted her to alert him so he could beat the coward to a bloody pulp.

"I don't have any bad intention against them," she said. "Our prayer is that they should understand what they are doing is not good, so that they will be saved when they die or when our Lord Jesus will come. Because if they died in this habit, they will not see God."

Forgiveness still is not easy for Amina, who trusts in God for justice. She clings to the words of the apostle Paul: "Beloved, never avenge yourselves, but leave it to the wrath of God, for it is written, 'Vengeance is mine, I will repay, says the Lord'" (Romans 12:19).

"I am pleading with God to give me a courageous heart, that he will give me patience so that I will not betray his name," she said. "I should hold on to God no matter the suffering or persecution. Every day I ask him that in all of this suffering he will give me courage, that nothing will tempt me to turn back from him."

Amina, like so many other persecuted Jesus followers, reminds us that we, too, can forgive people who have committed offenses toward us. Her prayers for the salvation of those who do evil are prayers that need to be on our lips. Her prayer for the courage to forgive so that we do not betray God's name is a prayer that needs to be in our hearts. Together, with our global family in Christ, "let us hold fast the confession of our hope without wavering, for he who promised is faithful" (Hebrews 10:23).

37

Forgiving Your Enemies Is Good

Diya
Somalia

A warm wind blew dust into the Somali sky, creating a brownish haze—just like most days. Fishing boats bobbed on the Indian Ocean beyond. Muslim women wrapped in colorful clothing walked briskly to market, their veils obscuring all but the roundness of their faces.

In a culture that believed some things must be covered up, Diya was a quiet rebel. Diya had trusted in Christ, as had his wife, Aniso, and their six-year-old son, Amiir. For nearly two decades, this Muslim-turned-Christian had gone against the grain of conventional thinking. He refused to hide his Somali-language Bible.

His decision was not motivated by pride. He loved this book for a number of reasons, and he felt no need to hide it away as is if it were something shameful. It was also one of his few possessions that survived a 1991 house fire triggered by the civil-war outbreak. Most important, it was God's Word.

Some of its scorched pages were still legible, and he read from them every day. His favorite story featured Abraham, who was going to sacrifice his son when an angel gave a ram to save Isaac's life. He also liked the promise in the New Testament that Jesus had become like that ram—a sacrifice for all of humanity's sin.

"When I read the Bible, I was reassured knowing that Christ is always with me," Diya reflected. That is exactly what he was doing when Amiir watched his father read the Bible and then set it aside.

Sharing his father's love for God's Word, Amiir took the Bible—with the big, bold cross engraved on its cover—and sat on the crumbling curb outside. He stretched out his feet in the dirt and opened up the book, just like his dad. As the morning bustle picked up, he watched passersby carefully in order to recognize the little boys he knew.

Suddenly, a vehicle pulled up near Amiir, kicking up a cloud of dust. Out rushed two soldiers, members of the Islamic Courts Union, a militant tribal alliance that controlled most of southern Somalia. Their motto: "There is no God but Allah; Muhammad is the messenger of God."

"Little boy," asked one, "where did you get that book you are holding?"

"It is Papa's," he replied proudly.

"And where is Papa?"

"Inside," Amiir said, nodding back at the house.

The soldiers knocked on the door. When Diya opened it, a soldier rammed the butt of his rifle into his head.

"Papa!" screamed Amiir.

Diya crumpled to the ground, unconscious. Amiir ran to him, wailing in grief. Aniso bent over her husband, one arm wrapped around her son to provide comfort.

"Why have you done this?" she asked, eyes ablaze in anger. She pulled her son to her chest.

Blam!

The bullet killed Amiir instantly, passing through his head and into his mother's stomach. She died later at a hospital.

Diya recovered and avoided arrest for having the Bible, but only because a tribal leader intervened on his behalf. Months later, he says the deaths of his wife and son have made him stronger and that he has forgiven the man who killed his wife and son.

"Loving and forgiving your enemies is good," he said. "I know my wife and son are with Jesus Christ. Everything that has happened has happened by the grace of God. And I am closer to Jesus than before. I don't have it as bad as some others. There are other people who have been through worse treatment than me. These things happen, and this is how we live."

Still, it is a struggle for him to care for his two remaining sons alone. He grieves for the playful little boy he lost because of his Christian faith. Yet he also longs to grow in his faith and love God as Abraham did when he was willing to give up everything for God, even his son.

Life in a place where persecution is as intense as it is in Somalia is extremely difficult. Diya and his fellow believers welcome the prayers and support of the global family of Christ to help shoulder the burden they carry. Jesus knows the heartache and challenges his followers face when they give up everything for him. It is those who are faithful in giving it all whom Jesus declares to be "worthy of me" (Matthew 10:37).

38

Giving Others a Second Chance

Awuna
Nigeria

At his volunteer job at a hospital in Jos, northern Nigeria, Awuna had just started his Friday shift.

"Awuna, I need you in the exam room," said a coworker.

"Okay, boss, I'm on my—"

Gunfire cracked. People in the room froze in fear. Thirty-one-year-old Awuna had heard gunshots before, but the sound and number of these echoed ominously. This shooting was serious—and close.

As other people scurried for cover, Awuna raced for his motorbike. Islamic militants had struck his village on the outskirts of Jos before. He sped down a dirt road that was eerily empty, hoping to make it to his home.

When he arrived in the village, a few miles from downtown Jos, he saw that it was under attack. *Wait*, he thought. *It is Friday—the day when the children are at the church practicing for Sunday's program.*

He stopped his motorbike and ran toward the church. Inside, children were screaming, shouting, and—oddly—pointing at a container. It was a harmless-looking powdered-milk can—except for the wire dangling from it.

His first thought: *Bomb.*

His second thought: *Children.*

Immediately, he grabbed the container, intending to toss it through an open window to his right.

Ku-wam!

The percussion of the blast slammed Awuna onto his back. Shrapnel pierced his body in many places. His mangled hands bled profusely. The last thing he saw before passing out was children gathering around him. Stunned. Tear stained. Unharmed.

For months following the explosion, Awuna didn't know where he was or the difference between night and day. He experienced excruciating pain. It took numerous operations to repair his badly damaged hands, but his wounds were not only physical. When the mental fogginess wore off, it was replaced with seething anger and a deep sense of bitterness toward those who had planted the bomb.

"I was angry," he said. "I didn't blame God, but I was thinking of vengeance—vengeance against those who hurt me."

Then something happened. Other Christians started coming to visit Awuna. They prayed with him and for him. They helped him read his Bible. As they stood with him, he forged a new life that was anchored in devotion to Jesus. His have-to-go-to-church attitude was replaced by a consuming zeal to learn more, live out the gospel, and spread the good news.

"Before the attack, I was not a strong Christian," he said. "But after going through what I went through, seeing other Christians go through suffering, and having Christians encourage me and pray for me, it all brought me closer to Christ. I'm more committed to prayer and fasting and studying the Bible. God gave me a second chance to live in the world, and I want to live it for his glory."

What about the anger, bitterness, and vengeance he felt toward those who had planted the bomb?

"If I saw them," he said, "I would tell them, 'I forgive you for what you've done.' We see in the Lord's Prayer that we have to forgive those who sin against us. Otherwise, our sins are not forgiven."

Awuna emphasizes that he is a changed man. The bombing set his life on a new trajectory. It gave him a second chance to heed Jesus's words: "If anyone would come after me, let him deny himself and take up his cross daily and follow me" (Luke 9:23). He is thankful he has a cross to bear for God's glory.

Because of God's grace, every day is a second chance for Awuna as it is for all who follow Jesus. By forgiving those who caused him so much harm, Awuna has the privilege of extending God's grace to others.

39

Extreme Forgiveness

Susanne Geske and Semse Aydin
Turkey

"Good morning."

"Morning, my friend."

On the sixth floor of an office building in Malatya, a Turkish city of half a million people, Tilman Geske and Necati Aydin greeted each other. They were soon joined by Unger Yuksel, the third partner in their Zirve Christian Publishing business.

Geske, a German national, had lived in Turkey for more than ten years. He was working on a Bible translation project. Aydin, a former Muslim, moved his family to Malatya from elsewhere in Turkey in order to plant a church. Yuksel was a Turkish Christian who had converted from Islam. The men knew that some Turkish nationalists viewed them as enemies who were working to undermine the country's political and religious institutions.

They began their day's work. Later that morning, the trio welcomed five young men, ages nineteen to twenty-one, to their office for a discussion about faith. The meeting had been requested in advance, but a discussion was not what the young men intended. Shortly after the meeting began, they tied up Geske, Aydin, and Yuksel, tortured them, and slit their throats.

The police arrived much too late to intervene. However, all five assailants were apprehended eventually.

The murders were shocking enough, but what stunned the Turkish people was how the wives of two of the murdered men responded. They immediately forgave their husbands' killers.

Soon after mopping her husband's blood from the floor, Susanne Geske told a reporter, "God, forgive them, for they know not what they do. I forgive the ones who did this."

Later, she explained her response: "I had not had a single second of anger or anything in my heart—nothing. Actually, 'didn't know what they did' is what came to my mind. Because the Lord forgave me so much, so I have forgiven them. Nonbelievers always say, 'How does this work? How do you do that?' I don't do that—this comes from the Lord directly."

In time, Susanne's daughters emulated their mother's response. At first, her older daughter was understandably angry, blaming the Turks and wanting to return to Germany. A few months later, however, she asked her mother if they could visit the assassins in prison. She wanted to pray with them, give them a Bible, and share Jesus with them.

Susanne's younger daughter, then eight, had similar thoughts. "Maybe they can become believers," she said. "And then if they die and come into heaven, they can tell Daddy and Necati and Unger that they are sorry."

Semse, Necati's widow, also was quick to forgive. "I didn't work to try to forgive them," she said. "God just gave me a gift."

She pointed out that forgiveness didn't mean she avoided feeling hurt over losing her husband. "I suffer a lot," she said. "I'm going to suffer until the day I die. But I'm not sorry for moving here. This was the best thing that could happen for Necati. He did a miracle; he did a wonderful thing. He created a very beautiful scenario of his life."

Seven years after the murders, the killers still had not been convicted. With a change in Turkish laws, they might possibly have been set free on bail. But Semse reminds us that this story is not about injustice. "This story is not a drama," she said. "This story is not about death. This story is about victory, gain, encouragement." She has heard about people who have come to know Jesus because of her husband's death.

"I know God showed his love to Turkey, not only on the cross, but by Necati's blood," Semse continued. "And how can I say, 'Why? Why do you give me this suffering or this cross?' I'm just asking God to help me to hold his cross and to lead people to help me hold his cross with me."

Truly our hope lies in Jesus, who forgives and opens heaven's doors for us. Let us rejoice in the extreme forgiveness we see in the examples of Semse and Susanne and her daughters and the impact for good they have created. May we support them with our prayers for comfort, strength, and encouragement as they hold up the cross of Christ in the face of persecution.

Martyrs in History

Richard Wurmbrand (1909–2001)
Sabina (Oster) Wurmbrand (1913–2000)
Eastern Europe

I don't wish to have a coward as a husband.

Sabina Wurmbrand, to Richard when he told her she would

likely lose her husband if he proclaimed Christ in front of four

thousand Communist delegates at a conference in Romania

Richard and Sabina Wurmbrand married in 1936, just as Dietrich Bonhoeffer was defending the Jewish people Hitler had in his crosshairs. The two were Germans of Jewish descent. Richard, intellectually gifted and fluent in nine languages, worked as a stockbroker and participated in leftist politics.

Two years after getting married, Richard and Sabina both became Christians, largely through the influence of a German carpenter, Christian Wölfkes. They joined the Anglican Mission to the Jews in Bucharest. Richard was ordained, first as an Anglican and after World War II as a Lutheran minister.

During the war, they preached in bomb shelters and rescued children from ghettos. They were repeatedly arrested and beaten and, at least once, nearly executed. Sabina lost her Jewish family in Nazi concentration camps.

After the war, the couple stood for Christ even though it meant certain persecution by the Communist Party. Richard distributed Bibles to Russian troops, and in 1948, the secret police arrested and imprisoned him. He would not be completely free until 1965. Meanwhile, Sabina was imprisoned for two years and forced to work as a laborer on the Danube Canal.

Ultimately, Richard and Sabina became known as "the voice of the underground church." In 1967, they began The Voice of the Martyrs ministry. But for all they accomplished on a global scale, their greatest legacy may be their penchant to forgive. In his book *In God's Underground*, Richard wrote about an incident in Romania involving a man named Borila, who was responsible for killing Sabina's family in a Jewish death camp in the early 1940s. Richard and Borila were introduced by their landlord. As they talked, Borila boasted about the huge number of Jews he had killed during the war.

"It is a frightening story," Richard replied, "but I do not fear for the Jews—God will compensate them for what they have suffered. I ask myself with anguish what will happen to the murderers when they stand before God's judgment."

Borila reacted as if he were going to pounce on Richard, but the landlord diffused the situation. Knowing the man loved music, Richard offered to play the piano for him. "I remembered how, when King Saul was afflicted by an evil spirit," he wrote later, "the boy David had played the harp for him."

After a few songs, Richard turned to Borila. He nodded toward the bedroom where Sabina slept and said, "Her parents, her sisters, her twelve-year-old brother, and the rest of her family were killed. You told me that you had killed hundreds near Golta, and that is where they were taken."

This time Borila looked as if he would strangle Richard, who then said, "Now let's try an experiment. I shall wake my wife and tell her who you are, and what you have done. I can tell you what will happen. My wife will not speak one word of reproach! She'll embrace you as if you were her brother. She'll bring you supper. Now, if Sabina, who is a sinner like us all, can forgive and love like this, imagine how Jesus, who is perfect Love, can forgive and love you! Only turn to Him—and everything you have done will be forgiven!"

Borila sobbed. For years, he had been consumed by guilt, unable to sleep, his shame covered by his boasting. "I'm a murderer," he managed to say. "I'm soaked in blood. What shall I do?"

Richard cried out, "In the name of the Lord Jesus Christ, I command the devil of hatred out of your soul."

Both men fell to their knees, then stood up and hugged.

It was time for the experiment. Richard gently awakened Sabina. "There is a man here whom you must meet," he said. "We believe he has murdered your family, but he has repented, and now he is your brother."

Sabina came out in her dressing gown, put her arms around Borila, and embraced him. Both wept. Then, as Richard had foretold, she went into the kitchen to make him supper.

Part VI

FAITHFULNESS

Therefore, my beloved brothers, be steadfast, immovable,
always abounding in the work of the Lord, knowing
that in the Lord your labor is not in vain.

1 Corinthians 15:58

Anyone who follows Jesus faithfully will pay a price for following him and holding fast to the truth of God's Word. It doesn't matter if we live in a community controlled by Islamic extremists who want to kill all followers of Jesus or a community where we have the political right to practice our faith but are social pariahs if we do so. Jesus knew it would be this way. He knew that the evil one would tempt us to doubt God, to fear circumstances, to choose the easy path over the difficult one, and ultimately to deny Jesus and abandon our walk with him.

It is not easy to be a faithful follower of Jesus when:

- Teaching our family, friends, and neighbors about Jesus can cost us our lives.
- Worshipping with our fellow believers invites wholesale slaughter by Islamic militants.

- Holding fast to our faith in Jesus and refusing to pledge allegiance to any other name results in beatings, torture, imprisonment, or death.
- Standing for the truth of what God says in his Word leads to scorn, hatred, and exclusion from our communities because it is not politically correct.

Yet God calls all who commit to follow him to be faithful despite the forces that oppose us. How is this possible? We remain faithful as we focus, trust, and rely on God, who is faithful to be with us and to reward us for all eternity. We also remain faithful as we support and encourage one another to be faithful *together*.

As followers of Jesus, we have the great privilege to pursue and serve God, not just as individuals, but as a family, the body of Christ. We have an important role in keeping one another focused on what is right and reminding one another of God's faithfulness. As Hebrews 10:23–25 describes, "Let us hold fast the confession of our hope without wavering, for he who promised is faithful. And let us consider how to stir up one another to love and good works, not neglecting to meet together … but encouraging one another."

What happened to Jesus followers when the apostle Paul was in chains is happening all over the world today! "What has happened to me," he wrote, "has really served to advance the gospel." Because of Paul's fearless faithfulness, "most of the brothers … in the Lord … are much more bold to speak the word without fear" (Philippians 1:12, 14).

Our faithfulness to God affects other Jesus followers. The faithfulness of one inspires others to remain true to God—to focus their hearts and minds on Jesus and face the temptations, endure the persecution, and risk everything to follow him. Will we stand with the men, women, and children who tenaciously cling to the hope that God will empower them to remain faithful despite the evil done to them?

40

100 Percent for Jesus

Ali and Rebekah
Iraq

It was March, the time of year when Mosul's insufferable heat had not yet arrived to bake the Iraqi landscape. In the coolness of the morning, the house was still bathed in darkness. Ali, a small man approaching age fifty, looked at his sleeping wife, Rebekah.

They were rearing three children together—Miriam, nineteen; Gabir, seventeen; and Amira, nine. Life had not been easy—not in Ali's line of work—but it had been a good life. God had provided, despite the war a decade earlier, despite the persecution they suffered for believing in Jesus, and despite their low income. Through it all, Ali and Rebekah had weathered much and had become especially close.

They lived a comfortable yet humble life in his parents' home. But household peace remained elusive because his Muslim parents were angry he had turned his back on Islam and become a follower of Jesus Christ. And they were especially angry because his family had chosen to follow his steps of faith.

As he did every morning, Ali tacked a handwritten note above the bed. It was a Scripture verse for his wife to start her day: "Unless a grain of wheat falls into the earth and dies, it remains alone; but if it dies, it bears much fruit" (John 12:24).

He walked into the kitchen. As was his custom, he picked up a dog-eared journal he kept near the toaster, looked up as if in thought, and began to write. "I am so full of the Holy Spirit that lives in my heart," he wrote, "that my small body cannot contain the measure of love he has given me."

Later, his family joined him in prayer. "Heavenly Father," he said, head bowed at the small table, "we pray that as I go out today fishing for men that the harvest would be bountiful. We pray that in this place that has turned its back on the good news, you will do a mighty work through me. Instead of facing Mecca, may people for the first time face you and welcome you into their lives. We pray that revival would come to Iraq. We pray that grace would come to Iraq. We pray that love would come to Iraq. Amen."

During the previous three months, Ali had led seven Muslims to Christ. His family also played a role in the men's spiritual development. Ali knew it was not enough to simply watch a man discreetly pray to ask God for forgiveness, acknowledge him as Lord and Savior, and allow him to enter his heart.

"He brought the first convert home," said Rebekah, "took out a basin of water, and washed his feet out of reverence and humility to Christ and as a reminder that he was a servant to all."

Going out each day to evangelize for Jesus in a city where people generally hate Jesus was not a boring routine for Ali. It was his life-blood. "We should go everywhere and tell people about Jesus," Ali told Rebekah. "I need to win one person for Christ a day, 365 days a year." Sometimes he drove to a site overlooking Mosul and with hands held high prayed passionately for the lost souls residing below.

Ali and his family knew the danger of his commitment. Days earlier, he had reminded Rebekah of that danger when he shared Acts 21:13 with her: "Then Paul answered, 'What are you doing, weeping and breaking my heart? For I am ready not only to be imprisoned but even to die in Jerusalem for the name of the Lord Jesus.'"

As Mosul came to life and the darkness gave way to light, he kissed his wife on the forehead. She bid him good-bye. It was the last time she would see him alive.

While Ali was conversing with a man on a street corner later that day, a car swerved to a stop by his side. Two men grabbed him, shoved him inside, and raced away. His captors tortured him for three days and three nights and then shot him nine times.

His captors and killers never identified themselves. No one ever asked for ransom money. Nor was anyone apprehended, which isn't unusual in situations like this. The Mosul police are not inclined to find the murderers of a man who preached Jesus. Clearly, they just wanted to stop him from spreading the gospel.

Wearing the traditional black garb of a widow in mourning, Rebekah said, "I never thought I would be living without my husband. He was my best friend."

Forty days later, as Ali's family and church community gathered to celebrate his life, everyone agreed that Ali would never have stopped sharing the gospel. During his years of evangelism, he had planted many seeds. He had introduced many converts to Jesus; these converts in turn brought others to Jesus. The ripple effect went on and on. Ali was a faithful disciple of Jesus who made disciples just as Jesus commanded in Matthew 28:19: "Go therefore and make disciples of all nations."

"Sometimes God allows us to go through a difficult time when we lose a loved one," his daughter Miriam said at the celebration. "During these times, he teaches us how to grow in our faith."

The aftershock of Ali's death arrived soon. Ali's grieving parents blamed Rebekah for their son's death. "Your support of his preaching this Jesus was responsible for our son's kidnapping and murder," they told her. They forced Rebekah and her children out of their house.

Nearly destitute, the family of four settled into a one-bedroom apartment in a village outside Mosul. The move separated them from their church community, but Christians who helped the family were surprised by their sense of peace, acceptance, and stability. Gabir worked after school to help support the family. Miriam attended a public university.

Rebekah carried on, despite her losses. Sometimes she is overwhelmed with grief. Tears ringed her eyes as she recently talked about her late husband. However, when she described his passion for the Lord, a smile spread across her face. "I am stronger now in my faith," she said. "Sometimes women want to cling to their husbands. But to love truly is to let them go and let them do what God needs them to do. I have no regrets. Ali died 100 percent for Jesus. The only thing he left us was his heart."

Ali demonstrated this through his willingness to die while serving Christ on the front lines. Instead of living for himself and earthly things, Ali faithfully obeyed God. He recognized a far grander purpose to life and death. As he stood firmly for Jesus on earth, he never lost sight of heaven and eternity.

Rebekah accepts his death as more than just a personal loss for her and their children. It served to advance God's kingdom. She knew that her husband's life was not hers to lose; it was God's to gain.

May we pray for Rebekah and her family—and so many families like them who faithfully cling to Christ after their loved ones die for his name. They need our prayers that they will find comfort in God's arms and not sink into bitterness. That they, like Ali, will become seeds planted for God's glory that bear much spiritual fruit.

41

Our God Is Faithful

John and Mary
Afghanistan

The bunker in Afghanistan was dark—but just light enough for John to see dozens of snakes slithering toward him. It was the latest ploy by his father, a top Taliban leader, to torment him for denouncing Allah and following Jesus. When that didn't deter the young man from his faith, his father released a vicious guard dog on him. For eighteen months, the young Afghan endured his father's torture chamber.

"God gave me power," John said later, "and told me, 'I am with you.'"

The trouble began after John went on a pilgrimage to Mecca in Saudi Arabia. He went as a Muslim and returned as a follower of Jesus. During that trip, a man with a shining face and bright-white clothes appeared to John in a dream.

"My son," the man said, "I see that you are seeking after me, but the real faith is not in Mecca. I am not here."

As he continued his pilgrimage to Mecca, John was troubled by the hypocrisy he saw at every turn. The holy pilgrimage was tainted with moneymaking exploitation of the pilgrims. As John and thousands of others walked around the Kaaba stone in the Grand Mosque, the truth suddenly bore into his soul for the first time: *They are worshipping a rock! An idol!*

Then John had a second vision. The same man in white said, "Relax. I want to talk to you because I love you. If I tell you who I am, you will lose seven things. You will lose the Quran and Muhammad. You will lose your parents. You will lose your child whom you love. You will lose your relatives. You will lose your wealth. You will be homeless, and they will drive you from your country."

John also learned that if he didn't endure such losses he couldn't follow the man in the vision.

"If you tell me your name," John said, "I will believe in you."

"I am your God," the man replied. "I am Jesus Christ."

John returned home and told his father, "I don't believe in your Allah."

"You are an infidel!" he raged and began beating John. "If you speak to people like this, I will cut out your tongue!"

"I want to tell people," John answered.

"If you tell people you have become a Christian, I will *burn* you, your wife, and your little son!"

That's when he forced John into the bunker. It was normally used for detaining and torturing anti-Taliban enemies. Even after his father released him eighteen months later, John's difficulties didn't end. Yet he remained faithful to his walk with Jesus, and God worked powerfully in his life.

He ignored his father's demands not to share his faith.

He witnessed his wife, Mary, trust in Jesus after she saw a vision of the Lord too. He rejoiced when his entire family—except his father—came to Christ.

When Mary became pregnant with their second child, her father insisted that they name the baby Sayeed Muhammed.

"No," John declared, "he will be named Isa [Jesus]."

"Your husband is an infidel!" the man hissed to his daughter. "You should abort the baby."

She shook her head and proclaimed her own faith in Christ.

Her father slammed her face to the ground, shattering her teeth. Then he punched her repeatedly in the abdomen and dragged her to John's father, who joined in the beatings.

When Taliban leaders learned of these defections from Allah, they blamed John's father and ordered him to kill the couple's young son. When the mothers of the couple learned this news, they schemed to help John and Mary leave Afghanistan. They vowed to care for their grandson until the family could be reunited.

After they fled Afghanistan, John took Mary to a doctor, where they learned the bad news that their baby was dead. Mary might die too unless the fetus was removed. John was unable to afford the procedure, so he did the only thing he knew how to do. He prayed as hard as he could. The next morning, he was stunned to see Mary standing calmly, holding a cup of tea.

When they returned to the doctor, his eyes bulged in disbelief. "The baby is alive!" he exclaimed. "How is this possible?"

John told of his prayer to Jesus, and the doctor called the baby's life "a miracle." Several people in the doctor's office turned to Christ.

But John's father was not finished avenging the couple's defiance of Allah. He discovered their new location and ordered them to return to Afghanistan and recant their faith. If they didn't, their two-year-old son would be killed.

Seeking help to save his son, John met with many authorities, but to no avail. The couple's faithfulness to Jesus proved costly, as John's father turned the little boy over to the Taliban. He was killed. A photograph of his lifeless body was paraded on a Taliban website to ratchet up the fear among infidels.

John's father then killed most of his family because of their allegiance to Jesus. And Mary's father, after learning his wife had conspired to get John and Mary out of Afghanistan, killed her by feeding her rat poison. Through the anguish of these losses, John and Mary's faith did not waver.

Even though they had to move six times in eight months to stay ahead of the Taliban, John and Mary continued to follow Jesus. They were baptized, and Mary gave birth to a healthy son. John, who wants "more people to see Jesus," began an Internet-based ministry that no snakes, guard dogs, threats, or even death could stop.

Such faithfulness does not come from our efforts. It is rooted in the character of God, who is faithful to those who suffer for the sake of his name.

The book of Daniel includes the story of King Nebuchadnezzar, who compelled everyone in his vast realm to bow to a nine-story golden statue of himself or be burned to death in a furnace. Shadrach, Meshach, and Abednego, exiles from Israel, refused to bow to an idol. "O Nebuchadnezzar," they said, "we have no need to answer you in this matter. If this be so, our God whom we serve is able to deliver us from the burning fiery furnace, and he will deliver us out of your hand, O king. But if not, be it known to you, O king, that we will not serve your gods or worship the golden image that you have set up" (3:16–18).

God was faithful to miraculously deliver these men, just as he was faithful to spare John and Mary when they refused to recant their faith and John refused to worship a rock. Like this courageous couple, countless brothers and sisters in Christ need our prayers. We can join in asking that God will sustain them during times of danger and despair. Inspired by their fortitude, may we also remain faithful no matter how high a price we have to pay.

42

Fighting against God

Shahnaz and Ebi
Iran

In his apartment high above a northern Iranian city, Ebi angrily clenched and unclenched his fists. *How could my daughter do this to me?*

"Shahnaz," he said, turning to her, "you are just going through a phase. It is like your fascination with this Islamic prophet or that American musician."

"Father, that is not true," she answered. "I am a Christian. I am a follower of Jesus—a passionate follower of Jesus!"

His heart pounded harder. *I must remain calm.* He tried to convince himself that it was only a passing fad. After all, he knew that two-thirds of Iran's population was under age thirty. The young people were so impressionable. What would fascinate them next?

"My daughter," he stated carefully, "I am confident you will soon leave this passing fancy behind, as you have your other fascinations with the West."

"No," she said, "this is different. This is not of the mind. This is of the heart."

Ebi bit his bottom lip lightly. "I am not requesting this, Shahnaz. I am *demanding* this. I am your father! You will not shame me, our family, or Allah by embracing a myth we despise. You will leave this Jesus behind you!"

"Father, are you listening to me?" she replied. "For the first time in my life, I am *content!*"

He clenched his fists and kept them clenched. *How dare she turn against the faith that I steeped her in! How dare she risk humiliating me!*

He said nothing and did nothing. But for two years, he grew angrier. He grew angrier when he learned his daughter associated with a group of young people who studied the Bible. He grew angrier when he discovered that she was telling her friends about this Jesus.

Then he and his wife came up with an idea. They would fight Shahnaz's obsession with this Jesus by tempting her with love. Before she had been duped into this conspiracy against Allah, she had been in love with a young Muslim living nearby. They forbade her from marrying him, even though she desperately wanted him as her husband. Perhaps yesterday's problem would be today's solution to her misguidedness.

They invited the man and his parents to their apartment to discuss a possible marriage. When Shahnaz learned they had lied about her renewed interest in him, she cried and became angry. She no longer loved this man nor wanted to marry him. Nor did she want to embarrass him or his parents.

So she asked her father to talk with her privately. "I'm sorry, Father," she said, "but I am a Christian now. I cannot marry a Muslim. My life has changed. I have a goal to serve God. And you, Father, would be well to serve him too. He is different than Allah. He—"

"Enough!" He spit out the word harshly.

Later, realizing Shahnaz had rejected their son, the parents left with him in a huff. Now Shahnaz's parents were embarrassed.

"How dare you shame us like this!" her father shouted when their guests left.

As his wife walked briskly to another room, Ebi unfastened his belt, yanked it from his pants, and whipped it across his daughter's back.

Whack. She collapsed to the floor.

"Do you realize that I can kill you right now, and it is legal?" he shouted. "You are a Muslim who has become a Christian! You are an apostate! My reputation will be ruined because of you!"

Shahnaz cowered as he whipped her again, and again, and again.

"I am going to keep beating you until you get on your knees and renounce Christianity and return to Islam," he said, flushed with anger. Sweat gleamed on his face; he breathed heavily.

"Lord," Shahnaz cried out, "I do not want to deny my faith. Jesus, help me!"

As her father prepared to hit her again, something very strange happened. As if guided by some unseen force, he stretched his arm wide to the side and began whipping himself in the face.

Whack! Whack! Whack!

"Father?"

"I am a … bad … person," he said softly, his voice no longer laced with anger. "I am so dirty. I am so stupid. I am fighting with God."

Shahnaz watched in amazement at the puzzling miracle that unfolded in front of her.

Her father fell forward on the floor. "Please forgive me, God," he prayed, tears streaming down his face, eyes closed.

Having heard his body fall, her mother raced into the room. "What did you do? Kill him?" she screamed.

"Mother," Shahnaz replied, "I don't know what happened."

Her mother started punching the emergency number into her cell phone.

The man's eyes suddenly opened, and with great effort he raised himself up from the floor. "I do not need an ambulance," he said. "I know now what I really need."

He stepped toward Shahnaz, who instinctively stepped back. He opened his arms—and wrapped his arms around her. His wife stared in astonishment. Shahnaz felt the unexpected assurance that she was safe.

"Please forgive me," he said. "Now I realize who I am fighting against."

Ebi then told her about a vision he had. "As I was beating you, I saw Jesus with his left arm wrapped around you. With his right arm he motioned me to stop the whipping. He said to me, 'Stop beating her. She belongs to me.' I realized as I was swinging the belt that I was beating Jesus."

Weeks later, after many discussions with Shahnaz and other believers about the Jesus his daughter would not cast aside, Ebi humbled himself and accepted Jesus as Lord and Savior of his life. Now as Ebi looked down on the city from his apartment, he experienced the peace of God, a peace he'd never felt before and still could not fully understand.

He glanced at his watch. It was time to get ready. Guests would be arriving soon for the church meeting he and his wife had offered to host. They had joined their daughter, who had faithfully walked in the hope of 1 Thessalonians 1:6: "And you became imitators of us and of the Lord, for you received the word in much affliction, with the joy of the Holy Spirit."

43

Losing Family, Finding Christ

Alejandro
The Philippines

Alejandro looked into the mirror hanging in his bamboo hut. He liked what he saw. The only son in a strict Muslim family, he grinned at how he had honored his father by joining Islamic rebels. Now he had become a cold-blooded killer, a terrorist for Allah. He even killed Christians. *My killing*, he thought, *proves that I am a worthy heir.*

Little did he know that one day he'd look into that same mirror and see himself covered with a sheen of shame, no longer viewing his violent actions so proudly. "I was not afraid to kill anyone for the glory of Allah," he recalled. "It was easier to kill a person than a chicken."

Even killers have a conscience, and Alejandro's Christ-driven guilt finally made its way into his soul. Although he remained committed to his Muslim faith and family, he left the militant group and turned to secular work. He hoped to find satisfaction in comfort and pleasure.

Jesus once again tugged on his heart. A Christian man he'd met during his travels around the island of Mindanao, one of seven thousand Philippine islands, invited him to church. Alejandro initially declined, yet the invitations continued so he finally said yes.

At church, God shattered the mirror image Alejandro had of himself. He saw what he really was: a cold-blooded murderer seeking satisfaction through violence, power, and bullying. It was as if God were saying, "See yourself as I see you, as a sinner, yes, but as a sinner saved by my grace."

For the first time since he was a little boy, Alejandro crumpled into tears. "I was a tough military guy, an Islamic killer," he said. "I never cried."

That day he decided to leave Islam and follow Jesus.

When Alejandro told his father of his conversion, the man exploded angrily and waved a machete in his son's face. "A curse on you!" he seethed. "I will *kill* you!"

Alejandro fled from the family home and has not seen his parents since that day. Occasionally, he talks with his siblings, and they always tell him the same thing: their parents still feel deeply angered, deeply wounded, and deeply betrayed.

Alejandro could not sacrifice his new love for Jesus in order to reconcile with his parents. He had received new life in Jesus and an eternal perspective of himself and his purpose for living. He quit his job and enrolled in Bible school.

Four years later, when Alejandro completed his degree, leaders of the denomination who hired him sent him to a remote, abandoned church building. At one time, 130 families had worshipped there. That is, until relentless attacks by Muslim extremists drove them away.

To say that he faced daunting challenges to remain faithful to God in that situation would be a drastic understatement. The situation did not improve immediately. His life was at risk each day. At night he wore earplugs to block the sounds of gunfire and exploding grenades as rebels—as he had been—attacked nearby villages.

When he traveled to neighboring villages to share the good news of Jesus, he walked or rode a water buffalo. It was a humbling change from his terrorist missions when he led raids racing in on a truck or motorcycle. Through all the challenges, Alejandro remained faithful. The church body began to grow a little at a time.

While attending a Christian conference, Alejandro met other persecuted pastors. Those interactions renewed and refreshed him. He even experienced the joy of leading a Muslim, as he had been, to Christ. During the final evening of the conference, Alejandro conversed deeply with an attendee grieving the loss of relatives—a pastor, his wife, and children—who had been killed by Muslim militants several months earlier. Only God could bring together a former Muslim murderer of Christians to comfort and pray for believers who were suffering at the hands of Islamic extremists.

Alejandro, who has now dedicated his life to sharing the gospel message of Jesus, experiences daily the challenge the apostle Paul gave to Jesus followers at Colossae: "Set your minds on things that are above, not on things that are on earth. For you have died, and your life is hidden with Christ in God" (Colossians 3:2–3). The old Alejandro is dead, and his new life is in Christ. Pray for him, and for all of us who follow Jesus, to be faithful to the new vision of ourselves that only God can give. Only God can transform a life built on hate into one built on the eternal foundation of Jesus and his love.

44

The Faithful Servant

Parveen

Pakistan

Twenty-three-year-old Parveen worked as a live-in maid in a wealthy Muslim home. She earned seventeen dollars per month, some of which supported her family. As a Christian, she enjoyed spending each Sunday, her day off, at church and at her family's home where people often gathered to read the Bible. It was a good arrangement—until the Muslim family she worked for found out.

One Saturday Fatima, her employer, surprised Parveen with a demand. "Do not take tomorrow off. Come to work. I'll be having some guests over."

"Tomorrow is Sunday," Parveen reminded her.

"What is special about Sunday?" asked Fatima. "Why don't you want to come to work on Sunday?"

"Sunday is our family's special day," Parveen answered. "We go to church."

As soon as the word *church* was mentioned, Fatima's eyes narrowed. She said nothing but thought deeply. The next morning, she ordered Parveen to clean the house.

"I am preparing to attend church," said Parveen. "I'm late."

Fatima exploded. "Why do you follow Jesus Christ and call him the Son of God? Why do you go to church? It is not true that Jesus is the Son of God. Our holy prophet, Muhammad, is the last and loving prophet of God."

"But it is true that Jesus Christ is our Lord," Parveen answered quietly. "I love him, and I love to worship him."

Fatima's anger notched higher. "You Christians are third-class people. You clean our Muslim houses. We provide your daily bread. Who are you to deny our orders?"

Fatima slapped Parveen, then punched and kicked her, all of it accented with verbal venom.

"Your Jesus Christ is not the last prophet," screamed Fatima, dragging Parveen through a doorway. "You Christians should stop worshipping him."

"I will worship my Jesus Christ," said Parveen, trying to defend herself and silently vowing not to cry.

Fatima called for her two daughters and husband to join her in beating Parveen. They accepted her invitation without hesitation.

"We will teach you a lesson," said Fatima's husband. "Accept Islam. Say that there is no god but Allah and Muhammad is his prophet."

"I will not," Parveen declared, on her knees, trying to fend off their attack.

Fatima halted the beating and tried a new tactic. "All right, if you accept Islam, we will provide you with a hundred thousand rupees. You can use this money to satisfy your family's needs."

Parveen looked up and shook her head. "If you offer me ten billion rupees, I will not accept Islam."

Quickly, Fatima switched to another motivational ploy. "If you don't accept Islam, we will beat you severely and blame you for stealing our money and for blaspheming the prophet Muhammad."

When Parveen refused to accept this deal, Fatima tortured her for three hours and then locked her in a room. Later, Fatima's husband and sons burned her wrists with cigarettes.

During the next two days, they gave Parveen only bread and some vegetables—no water. When Parveen's worried parents came to inquire about her whereabouts, Fatima said, "We have some guests, and Parveen is doing her work. Tomorrow she will be back home."

When Parveen hadn't returned by 6:00 p.m. the next day, her parents showed up with other Christians. Eventually, Fatima released Parveen.

Only on rare occasions does persecution of Christians in Islamic countries or by Islamic factions make the news. We may hear about a few instances of persecution that result in the killing of groups of Christians, but thousands of cases of subtler persecution are never reported. Parveen's story of faithful adherence to the truth of Jesus awakens us, as it did her, to the behind-the-scenes persecution many who follow Jesus face.

Her experience inspired Parveen to help other young Christian women who work behind closed doors in Muslim houses and suffer terrible persecution. After other Christians provided a sewing machine and she paid off a debt she owed Fatima's family, Parveen began teaching sewing classes. Her classes provide a way for young women to earn money so they do not have to work for families who would abuse and persecute them.

Parveen rejoices in her new opportunities for ministry. "Without any fear of being tortured, threatened, or verbally abused by a Muslim employer, at my home workplace I can pray and worship the Lord whenever I want. Hallelujah!"

Not only that, Parveen has found a way to support her persecuted sisters in Christ. When we consider how we can support the global church, our brothers and sisters who are in harm's way for their beliefs, we can pray that they will cling faithfully to the true hope of the gospel no matter their circumstances. And we can look for ways to stand with them as faithful stewards of God's grace.

45

When He Came to His Senses ...

Suleiman
Nigeria

In northern Nigeria, rumors about Suleiman Abdulai arrived home before he did. In the family's well-furnished home, his mother sat in a chair, working her fingers on each other as if kneading dough. His father paced. *This news is not true, is it?* they wondered. After all, they had raised him to be a devout Muslim. They had read much of the Quran to him. They had made sure that he understood the ironclad traditions of their family.

When he walked in the door, their coolness toward him could have chilled him to the bone. But he remembered that more important things were at stake than pleasing his parents. God's peace repelled his anxiety.

"Suleiman," his father said, after barely greeting him, "we have heard disconcerting news. Is it true? Have you given your life to"— he hesitated, as if reluctant to even say the word—"*Christ?*"

Suleiman nodded.

His father trembled slightly, "How much did the church give you to convert?" he demanded. His anger spiked. "How *much?*"

"There is no money," Suleiman answered. "I received the light."

His father stared disdainfully at him and then walked away. But he was not idle. He contacted every Muslim leader he knew and asked them to pray for his wayward son. But after a few weeks, Suleiman showed no change of heart.

"Deny this religion!" his father commanded.

"No, it is impossible," replied Suleiman. "I've found the truth."

Trying a new approach, his father sent him to live with a sister. She, too, rejected him, saying, "Perhaps you will come to your senses." She didn't realize that, like the Prodigal Son in the gospel of Luke, Suleiman already had come to his senses. As the passage says, "But when he came to himself, he said, 'How many of my father's hired servants have more than enough bread, but I perish here with hunger!'" (15:17). Suleiman realized that he'd been starving spiritually his entire life. Finally, through the love and forgiveness of Christ, he was feasting on Jesus, "the bread of life" (John 6:35).

Still, his spiritual turnaround had not been easy. Growing up, his intellect and sharp tongue made it easy for him to berate any and all who professed Christ. In fact, he specialized in humiliating them, believing that berating Christians would earn him favor in heaven. Then a coworker named Elizabeth invited him to a church service. When the service ended, he felt as if the pastor had been speaking directly to him. In fact, Suleiman accused Elizabeth of tipping off the pastor.

When Elizabeth denied doing that, Suleiman decided to create his own test. He sat far in the back during another service where he was sure the pastor could not see him. As the pastor delivered his message, Suleiman again realized that the message still seemed to be aimed directly at him.

"He said things that seemed to be specifically about me," Suleiman said later, "things I never told anyone before."

So Suleiman gave his life to Jesus. He began studying the Bible. He told anyone who would listen about his newfound faith. Despite his family's resistance, Suleiman married Elizabeth. When he took her to meet his family, relatives erupted in fury over the couple's faith in Christ.

"Deny this Christ or be killed," an aunt dictated. "Or at least pretend to deny the faith."

In the next room, where she could still overhear the conversations, Elizabeth trembled fearfully. She was certain that Suleiman's family members would kill her new husband.

Hour after hour, the family pounded on him with verbal assaults. Feeling himself wearing down, he remembered the words of Jesus: "Whoever denies me before men, I also will deny before my Father who is in heaven" (Matthew 10:33). Those simple words fueled his strength.

"I'm not going to deny who I serve," he declared. "I'm ready to die because I know Christ is here." He then walked into the room where Elizabeth was and took her by the hand, and they fled into the night.

Their persecution did not end that night though. Suleiman's family hired a mob armed with automatic weapons to attack the building where Suleiman and Elizabeth had rented a room, but the couple escaped. His parents disowned him and cut off all support for him and his wife.

Ten years have passed since then. Suleiman has dedicated his life to sharing Jesus with others. Suleiman and Elizabeth's children have never seen their grandparents. Sometimes his family situation has weighed so heavily on Suleiman that he has locked himself in a room and cried.

"I am not sad because I am missing them," he said. "I am sad because they are not going to heaven. They still believe that works will get them to heaven."

Suleiman clings faithfully to the God of the Bible and the Word. He knows that his hope must be in what God says, not in what his Muslim family or others believe. As the Prodigal Son story reveals, God stands ready to welcome home all who come to their senses and put their faith in him. We can rejoice with Suleiman because he found the God of grace and forgiveness. Pray for him and so many others in our persecuted family of believers who long for their earthly families to put their faith in the God of the Bible. Pray for him as he willingly reaches out to Muslims who have lost their way—as he had for so long.

46

The Irresistible Power of Love

Ehsan

Iraq

In the northern city of Erbil, a dry and dusty wind only worsened the pungent stench of burning trash and smoke from nearby industries. The smell of outdoor cooking announced another day unfolding in this gathering spot of refugees from war and violence. A mass of people sought shade in church courtyards and half-built or abandoned buildings. On the street, people propped up plastic, cardboard—anything—to shelter them from the scorching heat of the relentless sun.

Less than an hour's drive separates the better-known city, Mosul, from Erbil. Mosul is a conservative, Arab-majority city with a strong Islamist flavor. Erbil is a moderate Kurdish city that hosts refugees from all over the region: Arab Iraqis, Persians, Kurdish Iranians, and Syrians.

Amid this setting, Azhar prayed silently and gently brought up the subject of Jesus to his Muslim friend, Ehsan. He had talked with Ehsan about Jesus before, but his friend had resisted the gospel's good news.

"How can God, as you say, be both fully human and fully God?" Ehsan asked. Azhar tried to explain the concept, but his answer didn't satisfy Ehsan, who then brought up other concerns. "Christians killed Muslims in the name of religion during the Crusades, and the Christians I know are hypocrites. They preach lives of purity and live lives of impurity."

Azhar knew well the Bible's warning about hypocrites and how Jesus had exposed the hypocrisy of the Pharisees and others whose walk didn't match their talk.

"The Bible on which our faith rests condemns the very immorality you speak of," replied Azhar. "Not everyone who calls himself a Christian is a true believer."

Ehsan shrugged his shoulders, unconvinced, and their conversation shifted to another topic.

Azhar continued to pray for his friend as a new level of immorality swept into the region like a plague. Jihadists from the Islamic State overran Mosul in their attempt to establish a purely Islamic political-religious state. The jihadists gave Christians who lived in Mosul an ultimatum: convert to Islam, pay a high tax that virtually nobody could afford, leave the city, or be killed.

Many Jesus followers fled to nearby Iraqi Kurdistan, where Christian workers were already busy helping Syrian refugees and Iraqis who had been displaced during earlier conflicts. Others fled to Erbil. Amid the chaos and despair, Azhar and other believers did what God called them to do: serve others. They worked tirelessly to meet the needs of refugees in the region. As part of that effort, they stuffed plastic bags with food, clothing, hygiene items, and Bibles before distributing them to desperately needy people.

For two months, Ehsan, who had an office job, watched from afar.

"Ehsan," asked Azhar one day, "would you like to help?"

Ehsan hesitated, and then agreed to lend a hand. The team of volunteers worked for nine hours without even stopping to eat lunch. When they finished, Azhar invited Ehsan to join him for dinner. Midway through the meal, Azhar noted something different in Ehsan's disposition. It came out when Ehsan asked, "What kind of love do you have? What's the reason for this love?"

Surprised by the question, Azhar didn't reply immediately, thinking his friend might have further questions.

"Why do you include Bibles in these bags?" Ehsan continued. "And how can you love people you don't even know?"

Realizing that Ehsan's involvement with refugees had deepened his curiosity, Azhar replied, "Today you saw that there is a God who empowered us to work hard all day. He is the one who gives us this love."

Ehsan kept asking questions about the source of this love and then asked one more question Azhar had not expected: Could he have a Bible?

"I suggest you start reading in Matthew," Azhar said, handing a Bible to his friend. "If you get stuck on something you don't understand, pray and ask Jesus for answers. Call me in the morning and tell me about what you read."

The next morning, Azhar kept checking the time, eager to hear from Ehsan. But he didn't call. Worried, Azhar finally called him.

"My friend," Ehsan stated slowly, with conviction, "I have been up the whole night. Jesus revealed himself to me. I want to take the final step. I want to be baptized. I want to get involved in ministry like you."

When they met again, Azhar embraced his new brother in Christ and taught him all he could about the Christian faith. "There is no halfway commitment," Azhar emphasized. "The Christian life is a life of sacrifice."

Ehsan seemed to understand. He began attending a small house church in Erbil and was baptized. He continued to help pack supplies for the refugees. He prayed with those who received them.

Months later, a coworker of Ehsan's approached Azhar, knowing that he was Ehsan's friend. "What's different about Ehsan?" he asked. "There's a change, a new peace there."

"I'll tell you the reason," answered Azhar, knowing that Ehsan would want the truth to be shared. "He knows Jesus now."

Azhar invited the coworker to the weekly worship meeting. He came and, as the meeting ended, asked, "Could I have a Bible?"

Sometimes the need underlying people's questions about Jesus and the Bible isn't about finding answers and dealing with theology. It's about seeing the sincere love of Jesus demonstrated in places where that love is greatly needed. When those who follow Jesus take the gospel message seriously and live out God's love in their relationships, people who need Jesus can't help but notice. Jesus said that his love would make a difference: "By this all people will know that you are my disciples, if you have love for one another" (John 13:35).

It is our actions, not just our words, that cause people who do not know Jesus to ask questions and respond. Ehsan had heard the gospel many times, but it was actions that demonstrated the love of Jesus that moved him to believe. Love in action powerfully draws people to the source of that love: the God of the Bible. May God's love so fill our hearts that it will be evident in how we serve and care for others.

47

Seeking and Finding in Bangladesh

Pintu Hossain
Bangladesh

Pintu Hossain stood in front of the little brick church. In many ways, he felt like Joseph, the man he had read about in a Bible course, a man exiled by his brothers. Thrown into a well. Alone. Abandoned. Hopeless.

Yet Pintu was surrounded by crowds of people, a reminder that Bangladesh is the most densely populated and poorest country in the world. Pintu felt his heart pounding. *All these people going here and there*, he thought. *Where are they going? Why am I following them?* Then his mind switched to even more pressing questions: *Should I walk into this church? What about all the questions I've wrestled with since I was a child?*

In a country where nearly nine out of ten people are Muslim, Pintu had grown up believing Islam was the only true religion. He prayed five times a day. He fasted for thirty days during Ramadan. He encouraged others to pray with him in the mosque. *Why*, he wondered, *don't I feel content? Why am I not satisfied with my faith?*

Why haven't all my prayers and fasting assured me that I am right in following the masses?

During high school, Pintu had been fascinated by the idea of learning from people outside his culture. He began writing letters, hoping that recipients would write back. Some did. Corresponding with them became a serious hobby.

"Pintu," said a friend, "here is someone to whom you should write."

Its name, the Bible Correspondence Course, puzzled Pintu. *What is this Bible? What is this course? Is this the stuff of that Christian religion, the religion of idolaters who worship three different gods instead of Allah?*

But the offer, he had to admit, intrigued him. If he completed the Bible course, he would receive a free Bengali Bible. "Dear sir," he began, "please sign me up for your course. I would like to take it."

When the Bible course arrived, its stories only deepened his concerns about Islam. Here was a Christian God purporting to have created all people, to love all people, and to forgive them even when they sinned. Pintu completed the course in nine months and, as promised, received the Bible. Noticing what he was reading, his family members became angry. Just as Joseph's brothers abandoned him, so Pintu's siblings turned their backs on him. They believed he was being unfaithful to Islam.

Still, Pintu wrestled with deeper questions about life and God. He went to a local imam and asked, "Can Muhammad truly save me?"

The imam's brow furrowed. "What? Are you doubting our prophet?"

Pintu decided he would search for answers to his questions in the Quran. He didn't find any.

Finally, longing for truth and feeling curious, he stood in front of that church, a tranquil point in a world teeming with motion. He opened the door and entered, then quickly regretted doing so. The man in front, who seemingly had just started his talk, abruptly stopped speaking. The few dozen people in the room looked concerned.

The man started speaking again, from the beginning, but immediately stopped again. Now people began whispering.

For a third time, the man started speaking, and for a third time he stopped.

He is a crazy man! Pintu thought, retreating to the door in a huff. He had just opened it when the man spoke again, and his words went straight to Pintu's heart.

"I apologize," the man told the small congregation, "but each time I start the message, I keep sensing that God wants me to talk about another subject. About someone from the Old Testament. About Joseph, a man who was exiled by his brothers."

Pintu let go of the doorknob. He slowly turned around. *Joseph?* He returned to his seat, eyes riveted on the speaker.

As the man talked about Joseph and his brothers' betrayal, Pintu listened with increasing amazement. *This man is telling my story.* As soon as the meeting ended, Pintu rushed up to the speaker. "Do you know me?"

The pastor said he didn't.

"Then how do you know my life story?" Pintu asked.

Something clicked in the speaker's mind. "Now I understand why God did not allow me to preach my prepared sermon," he answered. "Today was a very special service, and I have been preparing for preaching a good sermon. But I heard a whispering sound in my ears, saying, 'Don't preach this sermon. Instead, preach from the life of Joseph.'"

Three times the voice had come to him, whenever he had begun his prepared sermon. Finally, he obeyed the voice.

"Now I understand it is because of you," he said, smiling. "God has brought you here to give you a new life through Jesus."

Pintu and the pastor talked for two more hours, discussing questions that had plagued the young man for so long. Slowly, he came to understand the truth about Jesus. He bowed his head and prayed for salvation.

Upon learning of this decision, his parents kicked him out of their home. But Pintu remained faithful to Jesus. He prayed fervently for opportunities to share the gospel with them and the siblings who had abandoned him. One by one, each came to Christ.

Without knowing it, Pintu had experienced this promise of Jesus: "Ask, and it will be given to you; seek, and you will find; knock, and it will be opened to you" (Matthew 7:7). He had been faithful to keep "knocking" and "seeking" spiritual hope. He sought God. He completed the study course. He walked into that church. Despite his uncertainty, he took those steps of faith—and God changed his life forever.

Now Pintu reaches out to Muslims who, as he did, feel alone, abandoned, and hopeless and who are looking for something more to life. He began offering a Bible correspondence course similar to the one he had taken that helped steer his inquisitiveness toward the resurrected Christ. He also started a Christian radio program. It is a great privilege for those of us who follow Jesus to stand for those who seek to know God. May we be faithful to continue seeking him and to obey his "whispering" in our ears.

48

Back from the Abyss

Mary
Nigeria

When the Islamic extremists Boko Haram poured into a Nigerian village in Adamawa State, villagers were terrified. Twenty-four-year-old Mary hid in a mud-walled house with her sisters and friends, one of whom was supposed to be married that day. They hid for days. Finally, at dusk on the fourth day, they bolted toward the bush, hoping to escape. Immediately, soldiers spotted them and surrounded the young women.

Mary knew all too well that Boko Haram's campaign to establish an Islamic territory in northern Nigeria had left thousands of people dead and forced more than 1.5 million people from their homes. She knew the insurgent group had kidnapped hundreds of young women such as herself—raping them, brainwashing them, and forcing them into their army as trained killers. She knew her own nightmare had just begun.

"The only thing I was thinking when they took me," Mary recounted, "is that I will die. I know they will kill me. I'm just praying to God everything that I do that is wrong, that the good Lord will forgive me."

Mary watched as the terrorists shot and killed her older sister because she had disobeyed orders to murder a man who refused to renounce his Christian faith. She watched as the friend who was supposed to have been married on the day they were attacked was "married" off to a Boko Haram commander. She saw her friend's two sisters meet the same fate.

And Mary was raped repeatedly. "Sometimes five men at the same time raped me," said Mary. "After this one, this one, this one."

When her captors learned she was a Christian, they forced her to recite verses from the Quran.

Week after week of such treatment took its toll. "I forgot how to pray, how to read the Bible," said Mary. "When I was with Boko Haram, the only thing was Muslim prayer."

Mary was forced to lead an attack against Christians who worshipped in her own village church. After the attack, the leader announced that she would soon marry the man who had raped her many times, the same man who had killed her sister.

Enough! Mary planned her escape carefully. One night when the terrorists were more drunk than usual, she and an older woman fled into the bush. When she made it back to her village, another wave of grief assaulted her. After his daughters had been abducted, her father died of a heart attack. She was the last living member of her immediate family.

Mary struggles to reclaim the young woman she was before the kidnapping. Processing the trauma she experienced will take time. When asked about her abductors, she says, "I forgive them, but if I catch a member of Boko Haram, I will kill him." It will be a painful journey.

But it is not a journey Mary makes alone. The body of Christ has come alongside her—expressing patience, understanding, and compassion as she tries to rebuild her life and as she chooses not to blame herself for what she or others have done.

Although she is not yet able to forgive the Boko Haram terrorists unconditionally, she is faithful in her walk with Jesus. "Before, I didn't go to church, I didn't read the Bible, I didn't pray," she said. "But now I go to church every day. I pray so that God will forgive me all my sins because I don't want to go back to my life in the past. I am now a born-again Christian. I am thankful for my life."

The writer of Hebrews portrays for us the perspective that helps all who follow Jesus to deal with the reality of their painful past and to thank God for his provision for today and for eternity: "But recall the former days when, after you were enlightened, you endured a hard struggle with sufferings, sometimes being publicly exposed to reproach and affliction, and sometimes being partners with those so treated ... since you knew that you yourselves had a better possession and an abiding one [in heaven]" (Hebrews 10:32–34).

The glorious hope for Mary and all of our persecuted family in Christ is that they will, with God's grace and help, reconcile the past trauma, live in the present, and anticipate an eternal, heavenly future.

Martyrs in History

Perpetua
182–203
Carthage (modern-day Tunisia)

"Father, do you see this vessel lying here to
be a pitcher, or something else?"
And he said, "I see it to be so."
And I replied, "Can it be called by any other name than what it is?"
And he said, "No."
"Neither can I call myself anything else
than what I am, a Christian."

Perpetua

For a woman of her time, Perpetua had lived about as comfortable a life as one could have. Born near the end of the second century into the privileges of prosperity and nobility, she was cultured and educated. In fact, the journal she kept about her trial and imprisonment is one of the few documents from the ancient world known to have been written by a woman.

By age twenty-two, Perpetua had married. She recently had given birth to a son and was still nursing him when she was arrested. She was preparing to be baptized as a Christian when the governor of Carthage began to enforce the Roman emperor's edict against conversion to Christianity. Perpetua was arrested along with Revocatus, the slave Felicitas, Saturninus, and Secundulus. Her baptism took place in prison.

Her father, who was a pagan, was greatly distressed by her commitment to Christ and the fate that awaited her. He tried on multiple occasions to dissuade her from holding fast to her faith. He begged her to "lay aside your courage" and consider the life of her infant son, who might not live without her. She grieved that her father did not share her faith and told him, "Whatever God wills shall happen. For know that we are not placed in our own power, but in that of God."

Even the Roman procurator asked Perpetua to consider offering some sacrifice to Rome for the sake of her distraught father and her infant son. At issue was her refusal to pay homage to the gods of Rome. All she had to do was throw a few grains of incense on the altar of a pagan god in recognition of its dominance and she would be pardoned—set free. She refused, recognizing Christ only as her Lord. As a result, she was condemned to death in the arena, as were her fellow believers.

While waiting for her sentence to be served, she was held in a dungeon, at times in stocks. At first the deep, oppressive darkness of the dungeon was frightening. She was troubled about her child until arrangements were made to have him brought to her, and then it "became to me as it were a palace." When the assistant overseer of the prison saw that the power of God was in Perpetua and her fellow believers, he allowed "many brethren to see us, that both we and they might be mutually refreshed."

One of her fellow believers, a slave named Felicitas, was pregnant during her ordeal. Roman law prohibited the public execution of a pregnant woman, and she was concerned that she would be prevented from dying with her companions in faith. They prayed earnestly for the baby to come early, and a few days before their scheduled execution, Felicitas gave birth to a baby girl, who was adopted by other Christians.

Even when Perpetua and Felicitas were led into the arena, they continued to stand strong in their faith. They refused to wear the garments of the Roman gods that were given to them and instead entered the arena in their own clothing. To the Roman procurator, they said, "You judge us, but God will judge you." At this, the crowd of spectators demanded that they be scourged.

Together, Perpetua and Felicitas faced a fierce bull in the arena. They were both injured but still alive. Perpetua lifted up Felicitas and held her close. To her remaining companions Perpetua said, "Stand fast in the faith, and love one another, and be not offended at my sufferings."

As the gladiators rushed forward to finish the job, Felicitas died. When Perpetua's executioner hesitated, she helped guide his blade into her body. As faithful believers in Christ, they had stood together and left this earth together.

The Word of God consistently reminds us that the world we live in here and now is not our eternal home. Those who believe in Jesus can look forward with confidence to our forever home in heaven, where there will be no suffering, only joy and peace. What's more, we are promised that any earthly persecution we endure in the name of Jesus will bring eternal rewards and the words from our Master, "Well done, good and faithful servant…. Enter into the joy of your master" (Matthew 25:23).

Commitment

Stories That Provoked a Response

These stories have taken us to places such as Egypt, Iran, Nigeria, Iraq, and Pakistan. We have seen biblical themes of sacrifice, courage, joy, perseverance, forgiveness, and faithfulness. The experiences of Samrita, Musa, Amina, Nadia, Hoda, Walid, Alejandro, and Mary are current and real, and they have inspired us.

We have read about the tears of these family members and perhaps even wept along with them. We have seen their joy and felt the hope that only an eternal perspective offers following the devastation they have faced. This overview forced us to ask ourselves, "What does it mean for *me* to be 'n' where I live?"

We need their example of faithfulness in the face of persecution. Their sacrifices are a powerful testimony to our loving God, whose grace reaches out to save every sinner and empowers those who follow Jesus to live in faithful service to him.

The pattern of joy that they manifest as they persevere and courageously serve Jesus inspires us and equips us to do the same. God is with those who are persecuted in a very special, intimate way. As we lift them in prayer, God gives us the privilege of being his hands, feet, and voices alongside them, no matter where we live.

What Is Your Response? Are You "N"?

You may be wondering how you would respond if you faced direct persecution. You may wonder if you've "got what it takes" to represent Christ well. We want to assure you that you *do* have everything you need to respond well. If you have Christ, you have everything you need.

In Luke 21:12–15, Jesus taught his disciples to prepare for persecution. He said, "But before all this they will lay their hands on you and persecute you, delivering you up to the synagogues and prisons, and you will be brought before kings and governors for my name's sake. This will be your opportunity to bear witness. Settle it therefore in your minds not to meditate beforehand how to answer, for I will give you a mouth and wisdom, which none of your adversaries will be able to withstand or contradict."

As a follower of Christ, we can be confident in this: No matter what we are facing, no matter where we find ourselves, no matter what kind of enemy we encounter, he will guide us—even the words that come out of our mouths. The promise is clear. God will be with you, and as you depend on him, he will guide you.

Now that you have been introduced to your brothers and sisters in some of the world's most difficult places, God will lead you to pray with them and to serve them. We don't want to turn our backs on them; we don't want to leave any of our family members behind. We will pull each other up. We will draw strength from their victories.

We will learn from their examples. We will expand God's kingdom with them.

We will keep our eyes fixed on our eternal hope in Christ, knowing that he is with us and that we are part of his eternal kingdom.

Our God is faithful. He will be with us and his Great Commission will be accomplished!

I Am N Commitment Prayer

Heavenly Father,

I have been inspired by my persecuted Christian brothers and sisters, and I ask that you will empower me to take active steps so I can grow in:

SACRIFICE. I will count the cost of discipleship and willingly pay the price because you are worth it.

COURAGE. I will not be paralyzed by fear because you empower me as I take risks to witness for you.

JOY. I will rejoice in the midst of my struggles and suffering in this world because of the eternal hope I have in you.

PERSEVERANCE. I will stand firm, resisting any opposition. By your strength, I will endure and overcome.

FORGIVENESS. I will allow you to work in my heart as I obey you by loving my enemies and forgiving others as you have forgiven me.

FAITHFULNESS. I will not allow adversity to cause me to be unfaithful to your Word or disobedient to your purposes.

Lord, help me be mindful of my Christian family so I will never let my Christian brothers and sisters suffer in silence, nor will I let them serve alone. I will let their testimonies inspire me to follow you. *I am n.*

_____   _____

Name   Date

www.i-am-n.com

Areas Where Christians Face Islamic Extremists

Major Groups and Hotspots

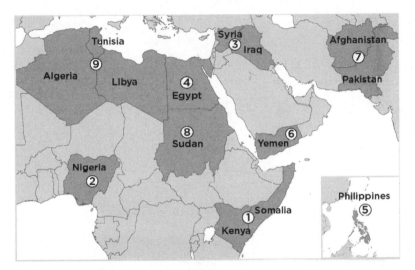

1. **Kenya & Somalia**
   Al-Shabab

2. **Nigeria**
   Boko Haram

3. **Iraq & Syria**
   The Islamic State (IS) (ISIS/ISIL)

4. **Egypt**
   The Muslim Brotherhood

5. **Philippines**
   Moro National/Islamic Liberation Front, Abu Sayyaf

6. **Yemen**
   Al-Qaida

7. **Afghanistan & Pakistan**
   The Taliban

8. **Sudan**
   The Sudanese regime led by Omar al-Bashir

9. **Algeria, Tunisia, & Libya**
   Al-Qaida and Ansar al-Shariah

Source: VOM, BBC News

The **Voice of the Martyrs**

The Voice of the Martyrs is a nonprofit, inter-denominational Christian missions organization dedicated to serving our persecuted family world-wide through practical and spiritual assistance and leading other members of the body of Christ into fellowship with them. VOM was founded in 1967 by Pastor Richard Wurmbrand, who was imprisoned fourteen years in Communist Romania for his faith in Christ. His wife, Sabina, was imprisoned for three years. In 1965, Richard and Sabina were ransomed out of Romania and established a global network of missions dedicated to assisting persecuted Christians.

Be inspired by the courageous faith of our persecuted brothers and sisters in Christ and learn ways to serve them by subscribing to VOM's free monthly newsletter. Visit us at www.persecution.com or call 1-800-747-0085.

Explore VOM's five main purposes and statement of faith at:

www.persecution.com/aboutvom.

To learn more about VOM's work, please contact us:

United States	www.persecution.com
Australia	www.vom.com.au
Belgium	www.hvk-aem.be
Canada	www.persecution.net
Czech Republic	www.hlas-mucedniku.cz
Finland	www.marttyyrienaani.fi
Italy	www.eun.ch
The Netherlands	www.sdok.org
New Zealand	www.persecution.co.nz
South Africa	www.persecution.co.za
South Korea	www.vomkorea.kr
United Kingdom	www.releaseinternational.org

Bibliography

BBC News. "Pakistan Minorities Minister Shahbaz Bhatti Shot Dead." March 2, 2011. www.bbc.com/news/world-south-asia-12617562.

Bonhoeffer, Dietrich. *Meditations on the Cross.* Edited by Manfred Weber. Translated by Douglas W. Scott. Louisville, KY: Westminster John Knox Press, 1998.

Bradford, John. *The Patient Suffering of Trouble and Affliction for Christ's Cause.* In *Writings of the Rev. John Bradford.* Philadelphia: Presbyterian Board of Publication, 1842.

Foxe, John, and The Voice of the Martyrs. *Foxe: Voices of the Martyrs.* Orlando: Bridge-Logos, 2007.

Ming-Dao, Wang. *A Call to the Church from Wang Ming-Dao.* Edited by Leona F. Choy. Translated by Theodore Choy. Fort Washington, PA: Christian Literature Crusade, 1983.

The New Encyclopedia of Christian Martyrs. Compiled by Mark Water. Grand Rapids, MI: Baker Books, 2001.

Stults, Roy. "Stubborn Saint: Wang Ming-Dao and the Birth of the Chinese House Church Movement." *Christian History,* no. 109 (2014).

The Voice of the Martyrs. *Iran: Finding Hope in the Axis of Evil.* Restricted Nations. Bartlesville, OK: Living Sacrifice, 2009.

Wurmbrand, Richard. *In God's Underground.* Bartlesville, OK: Living Sacrifice, 2004.

Wurmbrand, Richard. *Tortured for Christ.* Bartlesville, OK: Living Sacrifice, 2013.

Are You an "N" Christian?

To learn more about your persecuted family members and to get your church involved, go to *www.i-am-n.com/products*.